PRAISE FOR LOVE UNDER REPAIR

"*Love Under Repair* is a fantastic resource that will guide you through the overwhelming task of finding the right counselor to help your relationship. Informed by experience and research, Keith Miller walks you through the process of deciding about therapy by empowering you with knowledge, empathy, and hope."

—**Tina Payne Bryson, PhD**, co-author of the *New York Times* bestselling books *The Whole-Brain Child* and *No-Drama Discipline*

"Keith Miller does something unique for a book by a professional marriage therapist—he reveals his own marital struggles and endears you to him as he presents a clear guide to choosing a couples therapy that is safe and effective. His storytelling makes the many advances in attachment theory and brain science that he presents easy to relate to and understand. *Love Under Repair* is a practical tool that every therapist and couple should have within reach."

—**Harville Hendrix, PhD**, and **Helen LaKelly Hunt, PhD**, authors of the *New York Times* bestselling book *Getting the Love You Want* and *Making Marriage Simple*

"This one-of-a-kind book is a valuable consumer's guide to the world of marriage counseling. Miller walks alongside you, sharing his own story as he sheds light on a type of help that most couples seek out blindly rather than with knowledge and insight. This book will increase your confidence in making one of the most important decisions couples make—how to choose a good marriage counselor."

—**William J. Doherty, PhD**, author of *Take Back Your Marriage: Sticking Together in a World That Pulls Us Apart*

"*Love Under Repair* is immediately useful for anyone considering couples therapy. Keith Miller includes practical information on what to expect, on costs, and on how to get the most out of therapy. He covers three common couples therapy methods without bias and offers a clear path for the couple to decide which one is best for them. This book is especially useful for someone skeptical of couples therapy—buy it for him or her."

—**Wade Luquet, MSW, PhD**, associate professor of human services at Gwynedd Mercy University, and author of *Short-Term Couples Therapy: The Imago Model in Action*

"*Love Under Repair* is a very valuable book for couples who need help with their relationships. It's a wonderful introduction to couples therapy, which explains how [therapy] can help your troubled marriage, and how you can choose the best form of couples therapy for you. Keith Miller's writing is clear and easy to relate to, seasoned with many stories of couples' journeys in therapy."

—**Jay Earley, PhD**, author of *Self-Therapy*, creator of Self-Therapy Journey

"Never has it been more important—even urgent—to know how to form relationships that flourish. Keith Miller provides authoritative guidance for couples with disarming honesty and wit. At a time when we are surrounded by the devastation of divorce and cynicism about marriage in general, *Love Under Repair* is a well-written, scientifically robust, and easily accessible answer. If your relationship could be better and you want help, look no further."

—**Curt Thompson, MD**, author of *Anatomy of the Soul: Surprising Connections Between Neuroscience and Spiritual Practices That Can Transform Your Life and Relationships*

"Keith's gift to couples everywhere is that he has demystified the process of couples therapy. *Love Under Repair* is a clear and concise explanation of how to find a couples therapist who can truly transform your relationship. Couples at all stages of their relationships can now make informed choices about who to contact and what to expect from the best investment they can make in their relationships."

—**Jennifer Kogan, MSW, LICSW**, founder of DCTherapistConnect.com

"With compassion, sensitivity, and humor, Keith Miller serves as a hands-on guide for couples to find the best help for their unique circumstances. *Love Under Repair* draws upon Keith's own personal story as well as over a decade of clinical experience working with couples. I highly recommend it as a first, crucial step for couples who want to make the best choices to improve their relationships."

—**Joe Bavonese, PhD**, director and founder of the Relationship Institute

LOVE UNDER REPAIR

HOW TO SAVE YOUR MARRIAGE AND SURVIVE COUPLES THERAPY

KEITH A. MILLER, LICSW

LOVE GOOD PRESS

WASHINGTON

Love Good Press
1320 19th Street, NW
Suite 200
Washington, DC 20036
www.LoveGoodBeWell.com

The information in this volume is not intended as a substitute for consultation with healthcare professionals. Each individual's health concerns should be evaluated by a qualified professional.

Book design by Damonza.

Publisher's Cataloging-In-Publication Data
(Prepared by The Donohue Group, Inc.)

Miller, Keith A., 1977-
Love under repair : how to save your marriage and survive couples therapy / Keith A. Miller, LICSW.

pages ; cm

Issued also as a Kindle.
Includes bibliographical references and index.
ISBN: 978-0-9909169-3-2 (paperback)

1. Couples therapy—Popular works. 2. Marriage counselors—Popular works. I. Title.

RC488.5 .M55 2015
616.89/1562

For my parents, Roger and Elaine Miller, and for all my clients from whom I've had the privilege of witnessing extraordinary acts of love and courage.

AUTHOR'S NOTE:

THE NAMES AND scenarios described in this book, other than those pertaining to the author's personal stories, are based on a composite of many people and situations and are not the identities or stories of actual people. Every effort has been made to represent the therapies depicted here in a manner that is consistent with their typical practice, which includes wide variation from therapist to therapist. In some cases, the descriptions of therapy methods have been condensed or altered for clarity. Neither the author nor this book is officially endorsed by Imago Relationships International (IRI), The Gottman Institute, or the International Center for Excellence in Emotionally Focused Therapy (ICEEFT). The purpose of this book is to inspire interest in the subject of couples therapy and to provide motivation for taking positive action in your relationship or your clinical practice of couples therapy. It is not intended as a substitute for actual therapy, therapy instruction, or clinical supervision.

TABLE OF CONTENTS

PART I: Fragile. Handle with Care

Part II: Recommended Tools

Part III: Some Assembly Required

INTRODUCTION
LOVE UNGLUED

"No one—not rock stars, not professional athletes, not software billionaires, and not even geniuses—ever makes it alone."

—Malcolm Gladwell, Outliers: *The Story of Success*

THE QUESTION FROM the backseat startled me.

We were driving down the Capital Beltway near our home in Maryland, and I was busy trying to decide if we should do a "three-fer" and take care of all my errands at one time while the kids were in a state of relative non-chaos. We'd need to dash in and out of the grocery store, Target, and The Home Depot—tasks that could bring *me* to tears, never mind my kindergartener and his toddler sister, both with near-empty stomachs. I was pondering whether I should plan to have the kids melt down in the lumber department or in the deli when a small, bright voice disrupted the conversation I was having with myself.

"Is it true that you glue people back together?" It was my five-year-old son.

"Well, sort of...yes," I said.

Catching my son's eye for a moment in the rearview mirror, I marveled at where questions like this came from. It's as if kids—and this little guy in particular—have a Random Profound Thought Generator plugged into their motherboards.

My son thought about my answer for a long time. When we passed exit thirty-six, out came the follow-up question.

"So, Dad?"

"Yes, buddy?"

"What if there's more than one person that needs gluing? Do you glue them *both* together?" He was smiling broadly at the thought.

I was stunned into silence. Again I wondered: Just how did he come up with these questions?

My thoughts were quickly interrupted by a truck driver blasting the horn of his eighteen-wheeler as I drifted between two lanes in front of him. I never multitask very well, especially not when a five-year-old unintentionally highlights a big debate in the field of my profession. And certainly not while I'm also driving down a four-lane highway, my brain caught somewhere between provolone cheese, drywall screws, and my own marital issues.

I confess that the motivation to write about this subject wasn't just because it's my profession. If only it were that simple. A crisis in my own marriage brought me face-to-face with the decisions you're trying to make right now. My wife and I found ourselves confronted by a confusing maze of choices available to us when trying to find a couples therapist. If a marriage therapist didn't know where to turn when he needed someone to save his marriage, I thought, what chance did everyone else have?

THE COUPLES THERAPY REVOLUTION

We've entered an era in the history of psychology that's as revolutionary as when Galileo announced that the Earth rotated around the sun. For the first time in the little more than the century that psychology as we know it has existed, the broader health-science community has endorsed the belief that humans need other humans not only to survive, but also to achieve optimum physical and mental health.

Many of you will probably scratch your heads and wonder who would ever believe otherwise. Even a quick look at the long history of our species shows how we have advanced from hunter-gatherers to civilized societies because of our unique ability to build complex social connections. But the history of psychology has been subject to the same kind of fanatical devotion to "sacred" beliefs that Galileo faced. One of the longest held and most cherished of those beliefs has been that humans strive to be independent, autonomous, free thinkers.

Of course, this decidedly Western view fits snugly with our equally Western view of history and with the world influence we've enjoyed. One could argue that psychology's bent toward individualism and away from unhealthy unions has done the world a lot of good—its corollary in history might be how our Revolutionary War led to US independence from the

British Empire. So what happens when a prescription based on individualism—supposedly a good thing—is the only tool in the medicine bag of the doctor you call to save a marriage?

If you're seeking marriage therapy today, you could easily end up with a counselor who condones staging your very own "tea party." You could be advised to stand up to your spouse as if he were King George III, even before trying alternative, less reactionary attempts to reconcile and remedy the root cause of the relationship's problems.

Psychotherapy should always aim to help people find themselves, shed inefficient habits, and build self-confidence. Yet for the first time, a critical mass of psychology researchers and practitioners are questioning the mantra "Love Yourself before You Love Others." Psychologists and counseling professionals are now saying in countless conferences and publications: Wait a minute. Something's missing.[1]

---

1   The most dramatic example of the paradigm shift in psychotherapy toward attachment theory came in March 2010, in a stunning public confrontation between Jerome Kagan, perhaps one of the most revered developmental psychologists in the world, and Daniel Siegel, a psychotherapist, brain researcher, and leading proponent of the importance of using attachment theory in clinical practice. Kagan delivered a lecture that was highly skeptical and dismissive of the importance of attachment, attacking it as a misguided distraction from more important psychological factors such as inborn temperament and the human need to distance (differentiate) from others. Siegel, sitting in the audience of five hundred, darted to the stage—uninvited—and found a microphone. He challenged the shocked Kagan, "I can't let this audience listen to your argument without hearing the other side. Have you actually read the attachment research?" he demanded. The ensuing debate has lasted for years between the two, but it was a watershed moment that represented how the new guard in psychology, led by Siegel and others, had flooded the field with research and papers about attachment.

Today you'll find many psychotherapists promoting themselves as "marriage-friendly therapists." This label would have been heretical in most psychology circles twenty years ago, when marriage therapists were neutral about keeping relationships together and therapy was where especially bad relationships went to die.

In the past two decades, research has been amassed based on new brain science. This research shows that secure attachments to others—i.e. having healthy relationships—allows us to function at our highest levels as individuals. This "relational psychology" says the key to a healthy mind and body and to having freedom to explore independently, is to be "efficiently" but deeply attached to other people.

So when my son asked me from the backseat, "What if there's more than one person that needs gluing? Do you glue them *both* together?" I was reminded of the conundrum many couples face when seeking therapy. If you don't know the kind of psychology your therapist employs, it's possible you won't know whether he or she is using attachment theory—and you may miss out on the benefits it could hold.

This book came about because every day people blindly choose a couples therapist. This choice can seriously affect their experience and of course, their entire relationship. You could, without knowing it, hire a highly educated, experienced, and friendly therapist who would use techniques that are the equivalent of acids to help you dissolve the "sick" attachments you have to your partner. As you can imagine, implementing these techniques can result in the complete dissolution of relationships that are in trouble. What's worse is many therapists offer couples therapy but aren't trained to deliver this highly specialized treatment. Going to couples therapy today unaware of these startling realities is like asking your family physician to perform open-heart surgery.

This book will serve as a guide to help you navigate the range of couples therapy options available and will tell you how to hire a competent professional who can help you repair your relationship. As the head of a large psychotherapy private practice that specializes in helping couples, I know that people are often unaware of the vastly different kinds of couples therapy out there. Choosing the wrong kind of therapy for you is the fastest way to send your relationship into a downward spiral. But here's the good news: if you understand which type of counseling is the best fit for you and choose a therapist accordingly, you and your partner stand a good chance of benefitting tremendously. There are more effective and powerful methods of couples therapy available now than ever before.

I want you to have access to critical information about the differences in the types of couples therapies available. In the pages that follow, you'll get:

- A glimpse into the limitations of traditional couples therapy

- An understanding of how attachment-based couples therapy can help

- A fly-on-the-wall view of the three most popular "brands" of couples therapy available today

- Information about how to search for a therapist,

including questions to ask and an overview of cost and insurance issues

- A comparison of resources for couples, such as coaching, sex therapy, self-help, and weekend intensives

After reading this book, you'll have the ability to talk intelligently to a therapist you're considering hiring, and you can play an active role in your therapy by being prepared for what's likely to occur in your sessions.

PART I:
FRAGILE. HANDLE WITH CARE.

CHAPTER 1
GOING UNDER THE KNIFE

"Love is not an equation…It is not a contract, and it's not a happy ending. It is the slate under the chalk and the ground buildings rise from and the oxygen in the air."

—Jodi Picoult, *Vanishing Acts*

"HERE'S HOW WE'RE going to do this. Drop your pants and underwear so I can show you."

It's 8:20 a.m. on a normal Tuesday morning. I'm in a urologist's office. We're talking about how he's going to do a vasectomy on me the following week. Actually, he's the one doing the talking—I'm too busy turning as white as the tiles on his floor.

We've just met. Don't you think you're moving a little quickly? I try to form the words to a witty comeback, but I can't move my lips. *How weird is this?* Before I know it, he's grabbing me by the…anatomically correct place to make an incision.

"See how simple this is?" he asks, well inside my personal space.

Maybe from your point of view. But in case you're wondering, the right thing for anyone to do in this position, when your opinion is asked, is to agree. So I agree.

A week later, with the aid of a bag of frozen corn, I was on the mend. I didn't love having surgery, but I knew I was in the hands of a good doctor so I was satisfied with the results.

Personally, I think very intimate health exams are similar to couples therapy. Of course this is one example of how it can feel to visit any doctor—and one from a male perspective (I certainly don't envy what my wife goes through visiting her gynecologist). For you and your partner to really get the help you need when you're with your therapist, you're going to have to lay it all bare and tell it like it is. As a couples therapist, I'd worked with countless couples before I *really* got a taste of my own medicine and went to couples therapy with my wife. Even though a couples therapist doesn't have cold, hard surgical instruments, I felt as vulnerable as I had under the glare of my surgeon's bright examination lights.

THE BAREFOOT COBBLER

I never thought it could happen to *me*. I'd become the marriage counselor whose own marriage was worse than his clients'. I might as well have been an accountant who went bankrupt, a chain-smoking oncologist, or the cobbler without shoes.

You've heard of the seven-year itch that some married

people say they get? I had the three-year itch, the seven-year itch, *and* the ten-year itch. Each time I'd complain to my wife, "I can't take this anymore. Something has to change." But my wife and I had a way of riding over the inevitable waves created by these more turbulent moments. I tended to be the vocal one about feeling unhappy, and my wife knew that voicing my frustration was usually just my way of trying to work through the problem—not a sign of something seriously wrong. She would listen to what was bothering me and we could talk our way through it.

But then something happened.

Whenever I had one of my usual something-has-to-change rants, it would send her into a panic. "What do you mean something has to change?" she would reply. "You must think I'm not good enough." Trying to explain that this is only partly true was foolish—but I tried anyway. As a result we'd get stuck in endless battles, criticizing each other and feeling criticized. Neither of us could see the other's side. Instead, we'd get defensive easily and become irrational when trying to prove our points. (Just imagine Larry David from the HBO sitcom *Curb Your Enthusiasm* taking control of our conversations, but without any of the humor). It wasn't pretty. Complaining became so exhausting that I learned to stop complaining altogether. Of course that meant I was holding everything in instead. Then resentment would build and build, and my wife could feel that I was dissatisfied with something anyway.

"I can tell you're not happy," she'd say with an impatient raise of her eyebrows.

"No, I'm fine," I'd reply, my face a stone wall.

"You don't seem fine," she'd say.

That was my cue to get angry and blow up. I'd try to emphasize how "fine" I was, which of course only proved her point. And so it went. I learned it wasn't productive to complain or to keep quiet. The only obvious option left was to feel miserable.

It hadn't always been this way. I'd classify all but two of our fourteen years of marriage as very happy and incredibly rewarding. My wife and I love each other deeply. But somehow those memories were little comfort when it was all hitting the fan. As they say, things would've been going great, if only they weren't going so bad.

Marriage isn't a game, but in some ways it does seem like a sport. In sports, we often play to be the last one standing, to win. Sure, we may say we're happy with moral victories, with giving it our personal best. When it came to my own marriage, I knew I couldn't be content simply to have given it my personal best for a decade only to lose—to watch it collapse. Both of us were aware that we were losing something—letting it slip right through our fingers—something incredibly precious that had been built meticulously over many years.

One of the lessons my wife and I had learned during an earlier round of couples therapy we undertook during relatively peaceful times is this: marital fitness is just like physical fitness. Intimacy, it turns out, needs to be exercised regularly. Use it or lose it. Our marital fitness peaked around the time I became a newly minted couples therapist, eagerly trying out advice I was learning about how to handle differences and how to keep the embers of love alive. I even got my wife to go to a weekend marriage retreat, and we later joined an intimate group of other couples therapists and their spouses to talk about our marriages and to help one another. Each couple had identified healthy outlets to keep them from feeling overwhelmed.

But then my wife and I had kids. Our "fitness" routine went out the window. Our world got so much smaller, the way it does for most new parents. The healthy outlets—the friendships and routines that kept us stimulated and balanced—were no longer easy to maintain. I was already hyper-stressed from trying to be the breadwinner, but my fledgling private practice was not yet making ends meet. Despite being blessed with the best children anyone could ask for, parenting two kids under the age of five was extremely hard on our marriage. Add it all together—young kids, new business, little marital exercise, sad social life—and our carefully balanced way of handling differences toppled right over. The gloves came off. We hurt each other on purpose by saying things we never would have imagined saying before. We'd gone beyond being out of sync. Our respect and trust for each other had vanished like the warmth on a late-summer day when the sun goes down. It was getting dark.

ALIEN INVASION

We both knew we needed help, and, as a couples therapist myself, I knew what to look for in a therapist. I knew how it all worked. I knew that no two therapists are alike. I knew how to interview therapists to find what set each apart. I had an idea about how to sort through the jungle of confusing choices available for couples therapy and I could speak the language of couples therapy to our prospective therapist. I even knew that the best route for us was probably to use what's known as attachment-based couples therapy—something I'll detail later in this book. The only problem was—and this is hard to put in print—in all honesty, I was just going through the motions of looking for help. I had completely lost hope that anything could help us. In other words, it didn't matter what I knew clinically. Feelings—those tricky, hard-to-control, hard-to-predict things you get in your gut—stopped me dead in my tracks.

It didn't seem fair. During our darkest times, in the lonely middle of our emotional winter, we lost the sense we once had as a couple that used to point us toward each other like a compass, even if meeting halfway sometimes was a struggle. But now we were both very hurt, and our feelings had been shredded. Any therapy that would merely try to help us negotiate, apologize, or compromise would be doomed from the start. We needed a kind of therapy that could help us feel together—that's what attachment-based therapy aims to do.

I knew there must have been a therapist out there who had expertise in attachment-based therapy. This particular type of therapy is unique because, instead of bypassing feelings as many solution-focused approaches do, it works with your feelings. Only an attachment therapist could best help us slice away the cancer that was killing us emotionally as a couple. Yet despite the fact that usually I was that surgeon, I still freaked out. I panicked at the thought of another human really seeing inside my head and heart. Doing so requires a basic willingness to let go of control, something I had little intention of doing at the time. So, like most men faced with an obvious need for help and direction, I tried to do it myself. My "fallback" method of handling failure is to look for an answer as to why I failed in the first place. Since I began practicing therapy, I've evolved from simply turning to books or abstract concepts for answers to reaching out for help from people around me. In particular, my individual therapist has helped me a great deal. I've always kept his phone number within close reach. So when my marriage was on shaky ground, I turned to individual therapy before couples therapy. It held me together as a person and prevented my personal struggles from affecting the important counseling I provided to other couples going through circumstances similar to my own—which was, ironically, helpful.

During this difficult period, I focused on changing things that were within my sphere of control and letting go of things that weren't. I worked on being more patient with myself and negotiated with my inner perfectionist to find fewer things to micro-manage. But because my therapy was just that—my therapy—I was only treating half of the problem. At times I found inner peace of mind, but I was alone with that peace. Feeling peace with my wife wasn't as easy. In fact, the more I went the individual-therapy route, the more I was able to find peace and clarity just about everywhere *except* with my wife.

That's the major drawback of individual therapy or self-help. You can easily learn reams of information about your own problems, learn even more about your partner's problems, and maybe even understand the solution, but you're not mending your relationship *together*. You can learn a lot from making the effort to understand what might be causing your problems, but you must synchronize your work together, emotionally, as a couple to heal them. It takes a very skilled therapist, one who understands the complexities of the individual mind as well as the more mysterious rhythms of the heart (emotions), to launch a successful, all-out relationship recovery process.

In my case—and I believe this is true of many couples—therapy couldn't be about me and only me. Having a personal eureka moment is great. But at the end of the day, if my heart was still dead to the person that meant the most to me, no amount of personal insight could change the fact that I was a relationship zombie—I was completely unresponsive to my wife as a human. I needed a therapist who could feel into the void with us, and offer the steady rhythm of her own heart to lead us back to life. This is what attachment-based therapy offers—someone who is sensitive to emotions and skilled at getting them to be in tune between two people. We couldn't have needed it more.

THE WHITE FLAG OF SURRENDER

I decided that my pride and my own individual progress weren't as important as the fact that my marriage was slipping away from me. My wife and I told each other we couldn't go on much longer the way things were. With weary hearts, seeking relief at any cost, we talked about the "D" word the way

Harry Truman must have talked about using the atomic bomb. But divorce wasn't something either of us could really fathom.

That same week, my wife made me promise to look at a video on YouTube that she said spoke to her about our situation. Obliging her, I turned three shades of pale when I heard my own voice. She'd found a lecture I'd given about removing criticism from relationships. Pretty clever of her. By the end, my grouchy expression had softened into a sheepish grin. Internally, I began to raise the white flag of surrender. I wasn't going to avoid getting the help we needed any longer.

Calling 9-1-1 for your Marriage

But whom could we trust with so much at stake? The truth is that many couples don't stop to think about how to choose a therapist. Instead the arguments become so frequent, the resentment so intolerable, and the pain and loneliness so dark that many people make their first contact with a therapist when they're in the throes of a real emergency, like calling 9-1-1 when a house is on fire. I didn't want to bypass the important step of critically choosing who is most fit to respond with help.

If you've ever had to call the fire department, you've probably been grateful that they didn't fumble around wondering what to do once they arrived. I had to call them once, when the restaurant below my office had a chimney fire. Our suite has rooftop access to the kitchen's chimney, and the firefighters quickly realized they needed to go through our office to get to it. When the elevator door opened, six firemen equipped with axes charged toward me. I barely ducked out of the way to let them pass as I foolishly thought about whether to grab valuables before the office filled up with smoke. The firefighters were about to use their axes to bust through the door leading to the roof. I was so shocked and distracted that I almost didn't react. Somehow I managed to clear my throat and shout, "Hey! I have a key to that door!"

If your relationship feels like it's burning to the ground, no one would blame you, either, for wanting to get help as fast as possible. But what if you could get efficient relief *and* be confident that you aren't doing unnecessary damage in the process? The kind of therapy my wife and I got—known as attachment-based therapy—does just this. This therapy captures the moment-to-moment experiences you have during therapy sessions, and quickly helps you to turn expressions of distress into opportunities for connection.

I've written this book to share with you the three leading brands of this kind of couples therapy. I want to give you access to the doorway that leads right to where you want to be: in the hands of a competent marriage counselor with the right therapy for you. No longer will you have to feel stuck without an exit while your relationship goes up in flames.

BREAKING THROUGH WITH ATTACHMENT-BASED COUPLES THERAPY

My wife and I were lucky that we got help when we did. According to leading research about couples, once the cascade of negativity starts its ominous slide in your relationship, it doesn't reverse course without corrective intervention. But not all interventions are created equal. And not all interventions are delivered with the same quality.

My wife and I gave our therapist, Karla, some serious knots to deal with, but we believed her when she told us we would be able to untangle them together. By taking the time to learn about each of us as individuals, Karla decoded our attachment styles—when and why we turned toward or away from each other—and translated into simple terms what was ordinarily a vast and confusing array of chain reactions between us. She used her own warmth and careful attunement to the subtlest shifts in our tone or demeanor to literally *feel with us.* In a sense, she let herself attach emotionally to us and to our story—this helped her to help us relax and let our guards down. Almost immediately, each of us could feel weight being lifted off of our shoulders. Week after week for six months we hauled ourselves to her office to get doses of our "medicine." Karla took charge of leading us through a process that gradually filled in the deep ruts we had created in our behavior patterns toward each other. Each session allowed us to shed a layer of defensiveness or hostility, and revealed our softer and kinder sides. We gradually took greater and greater risks to reach toward each other, and made fewer demands. A new chapter was opening up in our marriage.

There was no one gleaming "aha!" moment. My wife never came through the doors and pronounced that I had been right about everything. Instead, there was a series of what seemed like a thousand little mercies, tiny glimmers of light that flickered in the shadows, where some of our darkest fears abided.

There was a correlation between going to therapy more and fighting less. Resentment gave way to deeper feelings of appreciation, as we learned again how similar we were. We recognized that, beneath the hard exteriors that nearly squeezed the life out of a very good relationship, we were both human and fragile. The sun was out again.

The truth is that our relationship was able to be saved by couples therapy because we didn't wait too long before hiring professional, competent help. Some research has indicated that most couples wait an average of six years after detecting a serious problem in their marriage to get help. For many, waiting this long is like pulling a parachute's rip cord when you're close enough to the ground to see your shadow—way too late!

I'm so glad that you picked up this book. It means you're just in time.

THIS BOOK: YOUR SECOND OPINION

My story may feel familiar. You might have been through therapy before and wondered, *What's the point?* Or maybe one of you seems more committed to working on the relationship than the other. Maybe you're emotionally exhausted and toy with the idea that divorce, at this point, might just be easier. Have you considered that you've been in the wrong type of treatment?

And if you haven't yet sought a therapist, how will you choose one? In our world, where concerns about insurance premiums, in-network providers, and co-pays trump finding the right doctors, there's a tendency for couples who are lucky enough to have insurance that covers counseling to reach out to the first person in their zip code who's on their list of preferred providers.

I believe that finding the right couples therapist should be given the same due diligence as finding the right surgeon. More than twenty years ago, my mother narrowly avoided a radical and invasive surgery that would've been completely unnecessary. She was told she needed her stomach partly removed to cure ulcers. Thankfully, she sought a second opinion and began antibiotics that saved her stomach and added untold years to her life.

Think of this book as *your* second opinion. I've looked at all the angles, both professionally and personally, and believe you'll save yourself time, effort, and money by using what you learn in this book when you're shopping for a couples therapist. If you find the therapist that's right for you, believe in therapy, and work hard, you have a very good shot at transforming or saving your relationship. What you'll find in these pages is a guide to understanding what I consider the most advanced and effective types of help for couples available to you today: attachment-based couples therapy.

I'll provide a detailed summary of the three most popular brands of therapy that contain elements based on attachment theory: Imago Relationship Therapy, Emotionally Focused Therapy (EFT), and Gottman Method Couples Therapy. This summary is based on my own experiences as a patient and as an attachment-based couples therapist myself. Finding a therapist doesn't have to be a confusing or overwhelming experience. The information I provide about these three methods will help you interview any therapist. You can cut out weeks of expensive trial-and-error sessions with therapists by having the basic facts about the leading couples therapies available to you today.

CHAPTER 2
WHY FEELINGS MATTER

"The ache for home lives in all of us. The safe place where we can go as we are and not be questioned."

—Maya Angelou, *All God's Children Need Traveling Shoes*

N O ONE WANTS to flunk out of couples therapy. In fact, many people who call my practice seeking relationship help tell me that I'm the last call they're going to make before they call a divorce lawyer. They want to "at least try to work it out" one last time. It's all on the line, they say. No pressure! When I first opened my practice, I actually rented office space in a law firm. Some people walked down the corridor to my office, past the lawyers, and said they hoped—half-joking—that the juxtaposition of our offices wasn't a bad omen.

The honest truth is that going to a couples therapist doesn't always make things better in your relationship. With the wrongly matched therapist things can go badly awry.[2] My stomach does nauseating somersaults when I hear those stories.

It's impossible to succinctly capture how attachment-based therapies compare to *all* other models of couples therapy. And keep in mind that most therapists mix and match therapy approaches in their practice. The following vignette is a simplified snapshot of many possible angles that could be explored about the differences between attachment-based therapies and one other popular type of therapy. You can use the broad brushstrokes I use here to start your own conversations and research into the finer differences among the choice of therapists available to you.

JACK AND IRENE FIND HELP

Irene and Jack started therapy because, as Jack put it, "If I have to wake up one more day like this, there's no point in waking up." The pain of living with Irene's machine-gun temper had become too much for him. Normally, when Irene's temper flared, Jack would retreat deeper inside himself, where his wife could never find him. He knew no way of protecting himself other than to diminish any sign of life, any sign of real human feeling toward her.

---

2   One thing that nearly all therapists will agree on is that in cases of clear physical or emotional abuse, couples therapy is not always recommended— unless you're working with a *team* of specialized therapists to safely provide a higher level of care. The same can be true when active, untreated substance abuse or mental illness is part of the equation.

Jack's vanishing act was also his way of protecting Irene. He knew that if he were going to react when she became angry, it would be with an overwhelming storm of his own anger. But he refused to allow his anger to hurt someone else. Growing up, he'd witnessed his stepfather physically and verbally abuse his mother. Witnessing this violence and being unable to stop it was excruciating for him as a boy. Jack came to believe that feelings are unwieldy, usually cause a lot of trouble, and are sometimes very dangerous. By the time he reached adulthood, he had learned to tamp down his anxious emotions and constantly lower his expectations. Life was more predictable that way. It wasn't anything Jack consciously tried to do—in fact, he often wished he could live a more carefree life. But he could only find comfort in predictability and routine, even if that meant he cut short his own opportunities and limited relationships with others who were fond of him.

One day, something got through to Jack. And it wasn't Irene. He watched a couple appear on the *Dr. Phil* show to discuss the discontent in their marriage. I believe that program captured Jack's attention because he wanted help. But he had shut down his feelings to the extent that he could no longer use his own voice to say, "I deserve better. You deserve better. We deserve to get help." The show spoke for him. The couple he saw reminded him of his wife and himself, and he started to wonder if there was someone out there who understood how to reverse the mess they were in. Much to his surprise, when Jack told Irene he wanted her to attend couples therapy with him, she agreed. "This much I know," she said, "is that I need all the help I can get to live with you."

The therapist Jack found through an Internet search was Robert, a cognitive-behavioral therapist (CBT). Jack told him about his growing intolerance of Irene's barrage of complaints and demands in one of the first sessions. "She always sounds mad at me, and she just loses her temper at the littlest things. There's no room for error on my part." Right on cue, Irene fidgeted with frustration and snapped, "It's because he makes me so mad all the time, and it's not over little things. He's so oblivious!"

Throughout the session, they constantly disagreed. They would nitpick, talk over each other, interrupt, and show signs of contempt (i.e. eye rolling). Robert listened passively for much of the time, seeming powerless to do anything except let the couple struggle. Finally, he intervened. "How's this working for you?" he probed, with sarcasm in his voice. Both agreed it wasn't. Robert went on to explain how he believed that feelings, especially painful feelings related to past events between them, were to blame for most of the turmoil in the relationship. He wanted to put Jack and Irene on an emotional diet of sorts, especially Irene. During their sessions, Robert said, they weren't going to waste time and money talking excessively about feelings, because, as was clear from their first twenty minutes together, they obviously weren't able to talk about feelings in a productive way.[3] So for the next ten weeks, Robert focused their sessions on behavioral change. He wanted to alter their bad habits and calm negative or

---

3   Some cognitive-behavioral therapists argue (as do some psychodynamic and family systems therapists) that they *do* pay attention to feelings, build an alliance with clients, and let them reprocess events from the past. However, cognitive-behavior therapy, psychoanalysis, and family systems therapy handle these three tasks in vastly different ways.

overwhelming feelings by changing their thoughts (cognition) and taking positive action to curb the bad behavior.

KEEPING SCORE—JACK: 1, IRENE: 0

With Robert's help, Jack and Irene designed clear goals for progress. One of Robert's suggestions was to have the couple keep worksheets where they were to note faulty ways of thinking (false assumptions). This included keeping a tally of positive thoughts or actions they used to counteract each negative thought or problem behavior. For example, when Irene wanted to give Jack a tongue lashing for how he kept forgetting about her Thursday night women's group meetings, she learned instead to identify the thoughts that were making her upset. Robert helped her label these as extreme and irrational thoughts, and he assertively challenged Irene to find positive thoughts about Jack to counteract these thoughts. Robert and Irene made a chart to keep track of how many negative thoughts she had. She wrote down things like, *He isn't there for me when I need him*, and *He's worthless to me*. For each negative thought she logged on her worksheet, she was to try to write three instances of positive thoughts she had about her husband. At first, she struggled to fill out that column. She couldn't bring herself to just flip a switch and reason herself into feeling positive. It wasn't that easy. However, she received a lot of prompts from Robert, who was energetic and convincing, and she finally went along with the exercise—partly just to make Robert happy.

Few couples admit that they "keep score" during therapy,

but almost every couple does. If the therapist takes your side on something, you score a point. If he takes my side, I score. By the time Robert finished analyzing Irene's negativity, Jack had scored the first "point." Robert concluded by suggesting, rather pointedly, that Irene's feelings about Jack were "out of whack."[4] He counseled her that if she changed her thoughts, changed her focus, and changed her behavior, her problematic feelings would cease to cause her such discomfort in the relationship.

IRENE: 1, JACK: 1

Then it was Jack's turn. He got the same treatment as Irene. Robert determined that Jack had a passively critical view of Irene. Jack assumed he was better than she was in areas that were important to him, such as household planning, time management, and driving. Robert found Jack's view of Irene unfair because Jack had almost completely shut her out of his emotional life, his routine, and his decision-making processes. How could he possibly be critical of Irene until he stepped up in the relationship, let his feelings be heard, and integrated his life more with hers? Robert chided him several times, saying "Irene's not a psychic. How is she supposed to know what's going on inside of you?"

Jack couldn't deny that he was withdrawn. Guilty as charged. But Robert wasn't paying close enough attention to

---

4   Many CBT therapists might use a fancier term other than "out of whack." CBT therapists have a catalogue of terms designed to debunk "faulty" thoughts, such as *arbitrary inference, selective abstraction, overgeneralization,* and *magnification/minimization.*

Jack to see that he didn't need to press this point. Jack already knew he was withdrawn and wished he could be different—but that wish was buried, hidden deep in a vault full of painful emotions. He had resigned himself to not being able to change. Ideally, Robert would have picked up on Jack's wish—even though he only hinted at that wish very faintly—and helped him nurture it back to life. If Robert could have provided a framework to bolster Jack, Jack would have felt encouraged. Instead, Robert delivered an impassioned "therapeutic" analysis. This not only "scored a point" for Irene, but repudiated a part of Jack that had been crushed many times before in life. At first, Irene hadn't liked Robert's strong opinions. But when Robert whacked Jack just as hard as he'd whacked her, she started liking Robert much more.[5] At least the score was now even.

Robert followed an aggressively cognitive model of therapy, so in his sessions with Jack and Irene, feelings were treated as untrustworthy and irrational. Even though I imagined that their therapist never intended his clients to feel this way, Jack and Irene told me "we felt bad for feeling bad...like *we* were the problem." They confided to me that their sessions seemed to be aimed at getting them to separate feelings from their communications and thoughts. Only then would their relationship improve.[6]

---

5   Not all CBT therapists are as blunt as Robert. However, among the adjectives used to describe CBT therapists, "persistent," or "confrontational" are sometimes included. In part, this may be traced back to Albert Ellis, considered by many to be the originator of CBT. Ellis was known for being a brash, no-nonsense therapist. (Ellis is usually named alongside Freud and Carl Rogers as one of the three most influential psychotherapists).

6   This view of feelings is a common CBT philosophy. Interestingly, the

After the second session, Jack commented enthusiastically to Irene, "This guy reminds me of that mediator I hired during the real estate dispute we had last year. He flat out told us, before knowing much, that he knew we were both wrong in many areas, and then he told us where we were wrong. He weeded out all our bull and got us to focus only on the things that could be proven from more than one angle." Jack valued solving problems efficiently in business, so initially he was really comfortable with Robert's solution-focused style of therapy.

The "mediation" style of couple's therapy is exactly what Jack and Irene were getting from Robert. He had a reputation for working with couples that many other therapists deemed to be lost causes. Because he didn't sugarcoat his diagnosis of people, he attracted clients who wanted immediate or dramatic results. He was trained to keep the focus of the sessions on the present situation, which he did with passion, sometimes forcefully intervening in conversations to keep Jack and Irene on task. His main goal was to steer them clear of subjective feelings on various topics, which tended to dredge up countless connections to the past. He tried to get them to focus on training themselves to think rationally and on acting in positive ways.

---

founders of Cognitive Therapy and Rational Emotive Behavioral Therapy (REBT), Aaron Beck and Albert Ellis, both referred to Greek Stoicism as the predecessor to the modern cognitive psychotherapy approach. The ancient idea of Stoicism is that emotional disturbance is caused by focusing too much on things outside our direct control, such as feelings, while neglecting things we can more easily change, such as thoughts and behavior (Robertson, 2010).

FLUNKING OUT OF THERAPY

Jack and Irene liked that Robert had "rules" for staying focused on what was fixable. Irene even joked that her biggest fear—that she would be reduced to a sobbing mess during therapy—had no chance of being realized in Robert's office. "I'm surprised he even had a tissue box in there!" she said to me one time. "Who has time for crying your eyes out when you have so many things being thrown at you to think about?"

Jack agreed. "I knew this was going to be intense, but going to Robert is really a major workout. I have to be on my toes and can't focus too much on the stuff that is tripping me up about us."

What Jack and Irene were noticing was indeed a change from the free fall they'd been in before starting therapy. They had clearly found a couples therapist who provided structure and guidance. And because Jack and Irene were both "doers," (Jack had recently completed his fifth triathlon at the age of sixty, and Irene had earned a law degree two years after retiring from her federal government post), they eagerly devoured Robert's steady diet of problem-solving exercises and behavioral adjustment plans. But Robert's approach put a lot of pressure on them to produce results. To meet the demand of Robert's regimented solutions, Jack and Irene needed to be highly disciplined. They made progress only if they stuck to the plan. Eventually, they ran out of gas. As Jack said one day, "It was like my first triathlon. I felt great during the first half, and then I hit a wall. There was nothing left. I was completely unprepared and couldn't go farther. There was nothing I could do but stop."

Robert was a skilled cognitive-behavioral therapist. While he did have many years' experience of using CBT with couples, the bulk of his training and experience was with individuals. He anticipated that Jack and Irene would show signs of stress after an initial phase of improvement. He acknowledged that the key to long-term success in treatment was getting the exercises to "stick" and become automatic habit. This wasn't happening, however, because Jack and Irene couldn't agree on what the problem actually was. Jack blamed Irene for being unpleasant and causing him to avoid her, and Irene justified her anger because of Jack's avoidance. Robert required them to follow a set of principles he provided on a handout that guided them on how to reach consensus by negotiating without blame. He suggested that they each offer up behaviors they were willing to compromise for the other to make a similar change, with no strings attached.

At first, this strategy seemed like a good idea to Irene and Jack. They agreed to talk about possible areas of compromise and to report back about how things went in the next session. When they came back the following week, Robert knew immediately something was wrong. Jack could only look at the floor. Irene looked like she was sitting on a bucketful of hot coals. When Robert checked in with her, she erupted into a tirade about how humiliated she felt. Jack had been empowered by the quick pace and success of the cognitive exercises to date, and had decided to voice his long-hidden fantasy of being more sexually inventive with Irene. He had assumed she would entertain the idea because she'd been so open to the other exercises—he thought she would be up for the challenge and dispassionate about the past. He'd been wrong. The only thing that Jack's fantasy aroused in Irene was scorn. He'd obviously stepped on an old landmine. All helpful-sounding exercises about compromise and negotiation were, in an instant, blown to smithereens over this sensitive topic.

Robert proceeded to draw up a new game plan that completely removed Jack and Irene's freedom to interact spontaneously during sessions. He now shifted into what Jack described as "professor mode." In other words, he became *even more* analytical. Rather than finding a way to acknowledge and help repair the hurt feelings on both sides, Robert did a lot of talking and offered lengthy opinions. From that point forward, as though Jack and Irene had flunked an invisible exam, Robert tasked them with answering lots of follow-up questions. His theory was that if they could explain the *reason* for their reactions, they could find a rational solution. Robert conducted four sessions of detailed assessment like this. He got into family histories and childhood experiences. Then he delivered his appraisal of the situation. Jack, he said, was suffering from the depression that ran in his family, and Irene's rapid mood swings pointed to bipolar disorder. Thankfully, Jack and Irene trusted themselves enough to realize that their therapist had gone too far. Irene later told me, "He wanted us to begin individual therapy before continuing in couples therapy, and he suggested that it wasn't a sure thing that we would even come back to couples therapy. We felt like this was the end of the road for us as a couple. Jack and I were devastated. We'd thought he could help us." At that point, Jack and Irene left therapy with Robert and called me for a "second opinion" soon after.

WHY SOLUTION-FOCUSED COUPLES THERAPIES CAN MISS THE MARK

Robert attempted to fix Jack and Irene's relationship before truly understanding the root cause of their problems. That is, he treated the symptoms instead of the disease. This method is fine if you have an ear infection, when you don't want your doctor spending days analyzing where the infection came from or why your family history made you susceptible to it. You just want to fill a prescription for antibiotics and get rid of it. But emotional ailments aren't that simple, despite our increasing tendency to turn to Prozac instead of talking to a counselor.[7] Emotions are useful parts of us, even out-of-balance emotions that lead to depression, because they're messengers that carry critical information about our needs and our history. And to a trained attachment-based therapist, depression is considered far more than a disorder—it's a window into your soul and a pathway to your most important life experiences.

Couples therapy as Robert practices it—not integrated with attachment-based methods—appeals the same way Prozac and other mood-regulating medications do. It seems practical. Simple. Neat. Achievement-oriented individuals like Jack and Irene love this type of therapy. But these methods seem to serve only as a Band-Aid in many circumstances. Jack and Irene could practice new behaviors or adopt the Alcoholics Anonymous mantra, "Fake it until you make it," but they

---

7   According to the Kaiser Family Foundation, spending on prescription drugs for mental health issues has greatly surpassed spending on counseling. In the U.S. between 1986 and 2005, 21 percent more was spent on prescription drugs than mental health outpatient counseling (2011).

wouldn't be making changes because they *felt* like doing it. They would be "white-knuckling" it, as addiction counselors sometimes say—making a change out of sheer will. But what do you do on days when you don't have any willpower and no one is there to tell you what you should do? Without a more nuanced way to deal with emotions, I believe many couples that engage in strictly solution-focused therapy run the risk of just going through the motions of change. They never tap into an inner motivation to change in a fundamental way. They fake it but *don't* make it.

New science about the brain says that whether we recognize it consciously or not, feelings are always involved in our behavior. Ignoring feelings and "faking" an attachment to each other, no matter how rational the plan, is bound to be doomed from the start. For example, Irene and Jack could spend months carefully practicing new habits to help them exile the negativity in their relationship. This works for a while. But all of a sudden, the negative feelings may spring up again unexpectedly, because they're signals of unmet needs that require compassionate attention. Jack and Irene's first therapist was authoritarian; he exerted maximum control with minimal warmth and openness to input from his clients. Jack and Irene needed a revolutionary kind of therapy to alter their seemingly certain path toward divorce. They needed a therapist who could be both methodical and open to their feelings and input along the way. I believed that their best chance for success was to follow the same attachment-based approach that saved my marriage.

I don't want it to sound as though I believe

cognitive-behavioral therapy or other solution-based approaches are *wrong*. But these approaches were definitely wrong for Jack and Irene. Their therapy with Robert made their problems worse, because although it increased their level of objectivity—normally a good thing—it didn't help them feel any more united. They could have completed every relationship exercise in the world and still felt miles apart. Their ability to attach was broken.

When Jack and Irene came to see me, they were hanging on by a thread. Jack was seriously talking about divorce. They were at least willing to try something very different from their last experience, however. I told them that, like Robert, I would offer them a lot of structure by directing their interactions, which would help slow down their reactions and keep the conversation safe. But unlike Robert who passed right over their emotions I'd be paying close attention to their feelings, teaching them that there's value in decoding emotions.

Jack and Irene were somewhat skeptical but still interested in my proposal. They breathed a small but noticeable sigh of relief when I told them that the conflict in their relationship was happening for a reason. Their relationship was not defective, no matter how much it felt that way. "Emotionally," I said, "the two of you make a lot of sense." It wasn't a rehearsed compliment—I really meant it. My training and experience in emotional intelligence with couples told me that their emotional reactions had a very sophisticated symmetry and purpose. My task would be to teach them how to respond to conflict without constantly working against each other. I had given Jack and Irene a glimmer of hope, and in return they extended their trust to me. On a most basic level—with the faintest signals of hope and trust—we three created an attachment. They trusted me and let go of a bit of control. Would it be possible to use that trust to repair the damage in their relationship and make substantial changes? I was about to find out.

THE DIFFERENCE ATTACHMENT-FOCUSED COUPLES THERAPY MAKES

Attachment-based therapy is very different from strict behavior modification therapies, which sometimes have the unintended effect of further depersonalizing an already depersonalized relationship. To-do lists and rational problem-solving exercises alone don't create the sparks needed to jump-start love that has flatlined.

Love and the more precise psychological term for it, attachment, is emotion-driven. Love is not based on logic, as anyone who has fallen into or out of love can attest. Since the central influences over inclinations to attach to certain people are not purely logical or rational, why do many couples therapies rely on cognitive, rational, or analytical methods to help struggling couples? Because learning to use rational thoughts to override spontaneous impulses *does* work sometimes in real life. Got a bad habit? The standard advice is simply to break it, to overwhelm it with other habits so it cannot persist. Feeling depressed? Make yourself clean one room in your house every day. Can't stop cleaning your house every day? Start volunteering and helping people in need. Can't say no to people in need? Start going to the gym to take care of yourself. These are simplistic examples, but they illustrate the point.

American culture is based on a "pull yourself up by your bootstraps" mentality, which resonates with some people but not others. Incorporating such a philosophy into couples therapy (as many traditional approaches do) assumes that both partners are two independent, autonomous people capable of applying rational thinking and problem-solving skills to their lives at all times. When I was having marriage problems of my own, I acted anything but rational. As a professional who also practiced for many years using strictly solution-based and rational methods for couples therapy, I can tell you that only couples with relatively minor issues were able to reap the benefits of rational-based therapy successfully. Couples with deeper problems require a different approach.

CONFIDENCE IN YOUR
THERAPY = BETTER OUTCOME

We've seen how and why using traditional, solution-focused therapy that minimizes the importance of feelings destined Jack and Irene for therapy failure. After their experience it's amazing that they didn't just determine that therapy doesn't work.

By knowing a little about how attachment theory has shaped the brands of couples therapy now available, you can determine which approach is the best match for you. If you're knocking on divorce's door, you don't have time to experiment. My wife and I didn't. Because I've used attachment-based couples therapy with the couples in my practice with great success I felt confident in it. So we went straight to an attachment-based couples therapist to get the help we needed.

As you read on to see how your situation might be helped with couples therapy, you'll also learn how couples therapy works and what to expect. That will help you believe in the therapy you're getting from day one. Many studies show that your own expectation about the help you're getting in therapy is, by far, one of the most important factors for a successful outcome.[8] You should walk into therapy confident that you know what you need and what the therapist can offer. Just by reading this book and spending time reflecting on what you need and/or expect to get from your investment in therapy, you're moving a step closer to healing and repairing your relationship.

---

8   B.L. Duncan , S. D. *Miller*, B.E. *Wampold*, and M.A. Hubble M. A., eds., *The Heart & Soul of Change: Delivering What Works in Therapy. (New York:* Thomson Reuters, 2013).

CHAPTER 3

CRAZY GLUE: THE SURPRISING POTENTIAL OF OUR ATTACHMENT TO OTHERS

"If you live to be a hundred, I want to live to be a hundred minus one day, so I never have to live without you."

—A. A. Milne, *Winnie-the-Pooh*

MY PARENTS CELEBRATED their fifty-year wedding anniversary in October 2014. They have glue. In the United States today, it's harder than ever to stay married. About half of all marriages end in divorce, and a divorce occurs roughly every thirteen seconds.[9] In some states, you can get a divorce without even stating a reason why. If

---

9   http://www.cdc.gov/nchs/mardiv.htm

there were a way to avoid this fate, wouldn't you want to know about it? Somehow, despite experiencing many of the same anxieties, fears, insecurities, and differences that cause some couples to conclude their marriage no longer makes rational sense, letting go of one another was never really an option for my parents.

The family difficulties my parents each experienced early in their lives would almost certainly have predicted that my parents' marriage would have been a disaster. But their love created a safe space for each other—a sacred sanctuary—that seemed to shelter them from the turbulence around them. They held on. They turned to God and each other for strength and comfort. They bonded to each other at their core. My mom might want to hold my dad's hand before a difficult doctor's appointment. Or my dad might open up to my mom about his difficulty finding a job after being laid off. They each see the other as a potential source of comfort, and are able to accept comfort. This isn't to say they don't have heated battles and major differences of opinions. They surely do. But through it all, fifty years later, they're still going strong. Science is now telling us all humans do better when we have someone like this to turn to.

THE NEW NORMAL: WHY ATTACHMENT IS ESSENTIAL TO YOUR HEALTH

Many couples therapists today—those not knowledgeable about the benefits of adult attachment—might quickly diagnose my parents as "codependent." This term implies their reliance on each other is unhealthy—a sort of addiction, like an alcoholic's need for a drink. The idea of codependency was developed to describe the way partners and families of addicts behave in concert, co-creating conditions that support using drugs or alcohol.[10] Those who believe that codependency is dangerous might tell my parents that they're too dependent on one another and need to create better "boundaries" in their relationship, to find ways to be more self-sufficient.

There's a parallel to this fear of over-attachment in the recent history of parenting philosophy in Western culture. Before we knew about the importance of attachment for children, experts often advised parents to be stern with their children, to show minimal empathy, and to avoid "coddling," lest they become "spoiled." None of these opinions took into account what we now know about the essential need for humans—of all ages—to develop and maintain secure attachment to others. If you have a "secure base," as a healthy attachment is sometimes called, you will be more comfortable to leave that base to explore. You're imprinted with the knowledge that you can come back to the people who love you for affection or affirmation whenever you need to. The way attachment fosters independence is known as the "attachment paradox." Secure attachment is crucial to becoming truly independent. Having a secure base doesn't make you clingy. In the best circumstances, it leaves you freer to be yourself.

---

10   This definition of codependency has been quite helpful to a lot of people and continues to be important to treating addiction in families. However, when applied too broadly to intimate relationships, anti-codependency doesn't help couples grow together.

To bring it back to my son's backseat question: "What happens if two people need gluing? Do you glue them both together?" We now know that adults *do* need to attach to each other, to be "glued," in a sense. But this "glue" that holds together couples like my parents, and my wife and me, is no ordinary glue. The attachment paradox seems to defy logic. Call it "crazy glue."

Through some recent discoveries in neurobiology—the study of the brain and nervous system—we're now discovering the true potential of human attachment in adulthood. We can now say conclusively that humans do better when they tend to each other's emotional needs throughout the lifespan. Maturity is no longer simply equated as having moved away from needing to be nurtured. Our brains are not mechanical processors that can function objectively all the time. In fact, our ability to operate as rational, objective people is *directly related to* having secure emotional attachments to others. If we're in close proximity to someone who's willing to devote time and attention to us and let us also care for them, our health and mental well-being is steadier and more balanced. Giving and receiving care, perhaps the very definition of love itself, is integral to staying alive. This is as true for adults as it is for infants.

We've learned through a hard trial-and-error process over centuries that everyone needs nurturing—infants especially. Did you know that in the 1940s, soon after modern sanitation practices at hospitals caught on, maternity wards separated babies and mothers at birth and kept infants in isolated cribs, away from "dirty" human contact? The surprising result was that mortality rates in the cleanest wards skyrocketed to more than three-quarters of all births. It became painfully clear that a baby's brain shuts down key survival functions when deprived of human contact and interaction—that is, *attachment*.[11] We now know that skin-to-skin cuddling, eye contact, talking, and handling literally turns on an infant's immune system and programs the brain to feel and regulate emotions.

Many studies show how being in a caring and committed relationship is good for your health. We've all heard tales of elderly widows who die only days after their spouse, but men especially seem to be affected by living alone. According to one paper published in the *Journal of Men's Health,* unmarried and divorced men have mortality rates up to 250 percent higher than unmarried women.[12] We're biologically engineered to engage in meaningful human contact with others. To be our physical and mental best, we need consistent and routine physical touch. We also need the emotional equivalent of touch, which is to be "in tune" or emotionally connected with others. Our world feels richer and full of possibilities when we're in the presence of others who "click" with us. We relax and are more open to receiving and giving help. These types of connections actually turn off the fear and pain centers in our brain. We communicate better and cooperate more. We feel joy more easily, play more, and get more work done.

---

11   Lewis, Thomas, Richard Lannon, and Fari Amini. *A General Theory of Love.* (New York: Random House, 2000.)

12   Daniel S. Felix, W. David Robinson, and Kimberly J. Jarzynka. "The Influence of Divorce on Men's Health." *Journal of Men's Health* 10(1) . (September 2013): 3–7. doi:10.1016/j.jomh.2012.09.002.

Aggressive impulses to fight our way out of or avoid problems are supplanted by a drive to explore and to find solutions. We enjoy greater health, and we treat the world and people around us better when our relationships—our attachments—are secure and healthy.

Positive social interactions actually alter our body's chemistry. Scientists have begun to measure molecular changes in our blood that cause us to be more efficient at problem solving and physical tasks when in the presence of a supportive intimate partner. In one important experiment, James Coan (2006) put test subjects into functional magnetic resonance imaging (fMRI) machines to study their brains' stress response before being told they would receive an electric shock.[13] Some subjects were allowed to hold the hand of a random person, while others could hold the hand of their spouse. Those in satisfying relationships experienced less pain and showed significantly less physiological stress in the fMRI scan when holding the hand of a loved one. Other research has speculated that being in close proximity to a supportive intimate partner causes the brain to process glucose more efficiently and prevents energy depletion. The key neurotransmitter thought to be responsible for triggering such calming effects is oxytocin, the same chemical released by all mammalian mothers and babies during nursing—it exists to help us form strong bonds.

We all get out of sync with our closest family members at some point. Attachment-based couples therapy effectively

---

13   J.A. Coan, H.S. Schaefer, and R.J. Davidson. "Lending a Hand: Social Regulation of the Neural Response to Threat." *Psychological Science* Vol. 17, no. 12 (December 2006).

retunes us to others and unlocks the natural functioning of our brain, helping it to balance itself. How does attachment-based therapy help us do this? First and foremost, it gives special attention to feelings. It targets the heart instead of the head. If you can speak the attachment language native to a person—the "buzz words" that make them feel valued and secure, show them the gestures and mannerisms that make them feel at home—then you hold the keys, quite literally, to their heart. You possess an uncanny ability to provide deep comfort by the subtlest expression of your own feelings. This can be from a touch, or merely from a look. Attachment-based therapy attempts to "rev up" the desire to bond and comfort and to slow down the impulse to turn away or attack. Rather than depending on carefully constructed logic and sheer conscious effort to persuade partners to mend their relationship, it calls forth a powerful inborn instinct to nurture and to be nurtured.

Some people find the idea of actively being nurtured, or actively nurturing another adult, quite unappealing. The memories and associations you have with intimacy may be such that it's the last thing you'd want to "rev up." That's perfectly okay. As the stories that follow will illustrate, love works in many surprising and different ways.

WHEN PBS IS THE ONLY CHANNEL YOU GET

When I was growing up, we had one television at home. Housed inside a vintage cabinet it was a piece of furniture unto itself. Our TV bore no resemblance to today's vibrant plasma-screened sets that receive hundreds of crystal-clear channels. Its single knob for tuning was almost unnecessary since it only received three channels that were clear enough to watch. One of them was PBS (WGBH, the Boston public television station).

When my dad watched TV, he watched PBS. Shows like *The Victory Garden, Masterpiece Theatre, This Old House, Julia Child*, and the endless humdrum of the *MacNeil/Lehrer News Hour* were nighttime regulars. The perfect torture for a kid! Sure, we snagged our share of the TV (after Dad started snoring). We watched shows like *M*A*S*H* and *Magnum P.I.* But I can still hear my inner eight-year-old shriek if I happen to catch a glimpse of Norm Abram, a host of *This Old House*, running his band saw like it's 1984.

Occasionally we'd watch a guy named Leo Buscaglia. PBS broadcast his motivational lectures about love and the powerful need all of us have for others. Compared to the "high drama" of Julia Child watching her boeuf bourguignon simmer (or as we would say in Massachusetts, "simma"), Leo Buscaglia was complete comatose material. When I heard his voice, I'm sure I made a point of serendipitously discovering that G.I. Joe was in grave danger and needed my assistance in the basement. Leo Buscaglia became known as "Dr. Love" because love was all he ever seemed to talk about. And he always told stories. He was so good at telling stories, in fact, that he had five books on the *New York Times* bestseller list at the same time. PBS discovered his talent for storytelling and his ability to captivate and inspire people and regularly aired his talks during their otherwise vapid fundraising drives.

Later, I would come to care much more about the kind

of things Leo Buscaglia spoke about, and the stories he told. To be sure, he had a certain charisma. You could see audience members welling up as he spoke. It even seemed that you could see the pores in his skin open up and drench the handkerchief he used to mop his brow. But there was an *element* of how he spoke—something you couldn't see, something intangible—that seemed to resonate deeply within my dad as he watched. And on one cold New England winter night, with the PBS special broadcasting into my living room, that element transported my Dad straight back to 1957.

INTO THE VOID SEPARATELY

Compared to today's sophisticated cancer treatments, state of the art medicine for cancer in 1957 seems downright barbaric. There was little known about how to slow or stop cancer's course. The first chemotherapy used successfully to put cancer into remission had happened just ten years earlier, and its horrible side effects either made patients wish they had died or actually killed them outright. Some doctors would simply tell cancer patients, "Go home. Go to your family. Go down to Florida for a long vacation. There's nothing more we can do."

In 1957, my father was fourteen years old. His mother had a habit of avoiding doctors, which made a person's already terrible chance of beating cancer completely abysmal. But when her normal monthly bleeding wouldn't stop, it scared her into letting her sisters take her to the hospital. When she was told that she had cancer, it wasn't even the beginning of the end but the end of the end. She died just two months later.

Sixty days whiz by when you know they're the last days you'll ever have to see someone. It's precious little time to say goodbye to your mom. And it's not enough time to bring a life to rest peacefully and to prepare a family—if anyone can ever prepare—for the emptiness that will follow. Two months is barely enough time to really absorb the momentousness of what is going to occur. When she died, it happened all of a sudden. It was a complete shock. During those two months, my dad would go to school, but he couldn't stay in class—he usually ended up in the bathroom hysterical, until his older brother took him home.

* * *

When my own mom was six years old, she woke up to loud voices and a scuffle in the kitchen between her parents. There was an argument. There was a gun. There was barely enough time for her to really figure out what was happening, and yet time seemed to stand still. Her brother, only two years older, got in the way to stop her father from hurting his mother and may have saved his mother's life. He was physically hurt.

My mother remembers the shock of that night as if it were yesterday. She was scared stiff, standing there in her pajamas and pigtails, peeking but trying to hide. Everyone survived, and her brother's physical injuries healed. But there was complete silence about the event. Not a word was ever mentioned about what she saw, how it felt to watch, or why it happened. Nothing. For some people, talking to others about the details of a traumatic event can make the difference between going crazy and making sense of something unfathomable. She and her brother didn't speak to each other about the incident until nearly fifty years had passed.

OUT OF THE VOID TOGETHER

The upheaval and uncertainty in my parents' childhoods were largely kept from me—until the night Leo Buscaglia told a story about a red dress. That story seemed to exemplify how my parents' bond grew and sustained itself over the years. They knew and understood that each had deep vulnerabilities. In other words, my parents have an inherent abundance of what attachment-based couples therapy offers to couples who are struggling: respect for each other's feelings. It comes from knowing where your partner has been before because you recognize that *you've* been there before. This kind of familiarity creates an intimacy that goes far beyond anything that can be exhibited in normal language.

The story Buscaglia told about the red dress is short but heartbreaking. A man's wife kept hinting to him that she wanted a certain red dress. She even ripped the page out of a fancy clothing catalog, folded it neatly, and tucked it into his shirt drawer. When her husband saw the paper, he set it aside, saying to himself, "Nice idea. Maybe another day." The birthdays and anniversaries came and went without a red dress appearing. Eventually the man's wife stopped asking. But she kept hoping that one day he'd remember. It would be even more special that way, she thought.

Years later, the man's wife became suddenly and gravely ill. She had only a couple of months to live. Toward the end, the man packed a small suitcase with enough clothing to last him several days and set off for the hospital to stay with her. He knew he'd be coming home alone. As he laid out his last shirt to pack it, he uncovered a paper, still neatly folded. There was barely enough time to acknowledge what the paper meant. She died quite suddenly. On the way home from the hospital, completely alone now, his first stop was at a fancy clothing store. At last, he made up his mind that she was going to look good in that red dress.[14]

I think I know why this story was so moving for my dad, and why he would tell it to my brothers and me occasionally over the years. It was his way of telling us never to lose track of what your loved ones mean, how precious that connection is and how it should never be taken for granted.

When it comes to finding professional help for your relationship, you might be one of the many couples that are easily attracted to the quick solutions offered by many therapists today. Perhaps you hope that there's a sanitized version of therapy out there that doesn't deal with uncomfortable feelings or struggles. Why can't we just talk about the *positive* feelings, you wonder? Maybe you're looking for a therapy that doesn't ask you to look deeply into yourself, into the story of you in your not-so-brightest moments of life. Don't. When my mom and dad created a love deep enough to last fifty years they did it, in part, by understanding each other's weaknesses. They found a way to repackage what they were given, to rewrite their family legacy. They, in turn, were able to hand their own

---

14   My retelling of Buscaglia's story undoubtedly differs in parts from the original as it's being related by memory.

children a brighter version of love that has unshakable roots. When I lost touch with that precious gift in the dark nights of my own marriage, there was a therapist out there who knew where to take me to get it back. But it meant delving deep into my own emotions, reliving the vulnerable moments of my life where I most needed love. She did it using her understanding of human attachment as a beacon.

ATTACHMENT: NATURE'S OVER-ENGINEERED SURVIVAL MECHANISM

From the day we're born, we rely on other people. In the late 1950s, British psychologist John Bowlby studied how consistent, nurturing human contact—or the lack of it—greatly shaped a child's ability to thrive. He and others developed what came to be known as attachment theory. Bowlby and others researched the correlation between an infant's attachment to at least one primary caregiver and the child's later ability to achieve social and emotional development.[15]

Childhood attachment theory soon became widely accepted; we now take for granted the idea that children do not arrive as miniature adults, but develop in stages over many years and require an environment that is consistently responsive to their changing emotional needs to become secure and successful adults. But it wasn't all that long ago that childhood as we know it didn't exist: kids worked on farms or were sent

---

15   I. Bretherton. "The Origins of Attachment Theory: John Bowlby and Mary Ainsworth." *Developmental Psychology* 28 (1992): 759. doi:10.1037/0012-1649.28.5.759

to factories to help support their families from young ages. Attachment theory is now so popular that it's hard to imagine raising kids in a world without it.

But if attachment is so critical to children, doesn't it make sense that attachment might be critical for adults, too? Doesn't it follow that adults must have their emotional needs met to feel safe, to be partnered in a harmonious relationship? Couples therapy and mental health treatments were actually much slower in adopting what's known as adult attachment theory. Until recently, in fact, "attachment" was considered somewhat of a dirty word in psychology. Older-generation psychoanalysts rejected it because it undermined the classic Freudian view that too much parental bonding with children aroused dangerous sexual drives in children that later caused mental illness. Behaviorists and solution-focused therapists disliked attachment theory because it put too much emphasis on feelings, which to them were seen as mostly or completely irrelevant to cognition or behaviors.[16] Even today, some psychotherapists still didn't really know what adult attachment theory is, let alone how to use it to effectively help couples.

Biologically, we've evolved to feel threatened when we're alone. Our mammalian brains have a kind of "redundant" engineering—there are multiple neurological networks that work in concert to make us highly social, interdependent

---

16   Classic behaviorism in the early days held some extreme views that radically minimized the importance of parental attachment to children. Renowned behaviorist John Watson said of children, "Never hug and kiss them, never let them sit in your lap. If you must, kiss them once on the forehead when they say goodnight." (Watson, J. B. *Psychological Care of the Infant and Child*. New York: W. W. Norton, 1928.)

creatures.[17] The next time your nerves are on edge and something makes you "snap" emotionally, remember this: you may think (rationally) that you're upset because your wife dumps her clothes on the floor and leaves them for you to pick up every week. It seems obvious that the source of your irritation is the laundry. But look more closely.

Your powerful-yet-primitive mammalian instinct to detect threats to relationships has hijacked your rational mind. The *limbic*, or emotional, brain feels a void between the two of you and sounds a visceral alarm, harassing you with distress signals that make you feel as aggravated as a baby that's been pulled from a mother's breast. You're not likely to realize that your irritation is coming from one of nature's most amazing instruments of survival. Your mammalian limbic system (emotional brain) is designed to sense disharmony between you and your most important attachment figures: the people who are special in your life. You probably just feel irritated at your wife ("I'm not your maid! Pick up your clothes next time!"), and think there's nothing more to it.

When you're emotionally agitated from the inside out, things you can normally tolerate or negotiate become major sticking points. So you argue about the dishes, or parenting, or your bank account. Of course, you can always find *rational* explanations for the tension you feel inside. But your outward awareness of irritation is secondary to the more primitive

---

17   Cultural anthropologist Helen Fisher writes that we have three distinct, powerful drives that ensure we find mates and reproduce: *lust* (sex drive), *romance* (desire for closeness), and *attachment* (desire for long-term union). Helen Fisher. *Why We Love: The Nature and Chemistry of Romantic Love.* (New York: Henry Holt, 2004).

emotional reaction you may not even be aware you're having. Unless you're looking for it (as an attachment-based therapist will), you might not notice the raw and often "yucky," uncomfortable feelings you get when someone isn't there for you the way you need them to be. As adults, most of us have learned to instantly disguise or to unconsciously numb ourselves to our innermost feelings of vulnerability. But these uncomfortable feelings are our primary and natural response to a disruption of attachment to someone important to us. Yes, the laundry habits are irritating in their own right. But the bigger feeling that's driving your frustration is that you feel like your secure connection to her is threatened. You need her to show that she loves you by not doing things that she knows bother you, and she's not responding. No matter how many times you try to tell yourself "it's only laundry," you can't let it go. It hurts.

The neurological "alarm" that goes off when you're in conflict with your partner is a function of how we've evolved to survive as a species. A major factor in our advancement is our ability to bond strongly to one another. Our discussion about attachment-based couples therapy requires that we define "attachment" more precisely. Attachment does not happen in just any kind of adult relationship—attachment is the bond you have to a special person. If that person is absent or if the bond is broken, you experience distress. We are sensitive to any signs of rupture of connection in our close relationships. Our need for each other isn't a weakness that needs to be tamed by logic and reason. It's an unstoppable, driving force that has allowed us to build resilient alliances with each other. Emotionally, we need each other as much as we physically need air to breathe. It's not a matter of preference for humans as to whether they want to be in relationships. Ironically, this need is why—as a species or in our own families—we fight, sometimes to the death, when our relationship bonds are stressed or broken. The fight is our way of protesting the potential loss of a vital connection.

"FISH THAT DON'T NOTICE THE WATER"

Research about human relationships is now coming forward to show that attachment to others directly affects your health regardless of age. An extensive study at Brigham Young University found that having social connections—with friends, family, neighbors, or colleagues—boosted survival rates by as much as *50 percent!*[18] Put another way, if you have poor social connections with others—a lack of meaningful, secure relationships—here's how your health risk compares to other well-known risk factors:

- Equivalent to smoking fifteen cigarettes a day

- Equivalent to being an alcoholic

- More harmful than not exercising

- Twice as harmful as obesity

Being in a relationship provides a clear health benefit, as

---

18   J. Holt-Lunstad, T.B. Smith, and J.B. Layton. "Social Relationships and Mortality Risk: A Meta-analytic Review." *PLoS Med* 7(7) 2010: e1000316. doi:10.1371/journal.pmed.1000316.

this and many more studies have shown.[19] Because the BYU study didn't factor in the quality of relationships sampled, the authors estimated that the 50 percent survival rate increase is a lowball number. That means if you have *good* or *great* relationships with others, your health risks would be diminished even more. In fact, a long-term study that tracked marital satisfaction and health over twenty years showed that when the quality of your relationship goes down, so does your health.[20]

Some people may find this hard to believe. One of the authors of the BYU study, Professor Tim Smith, thinks he knows why. "We take relationships for granted as humans— we're like fish that don't notice the water," Smith said. "That constant interaction is not only beneficial psychologically, but directly to our physical health."

Why is any of this important to how you choose a couples therapist? As adult attachment theory has taken hold in psychology, the major emphasis now in many modern counseling philosophies is that emotions must be respected and valued if they are to be useful in therapy. No longer are feelings something to be discarded or "gotten over." Advances in neurobiology have

---

19   A three-year study conducted by the Center for Disease Control on 127,545 adults found that married adults are happier, healthier, and wealthier than unmarried adults (Schoenborn, 2004). Wilson and Oswald (2005) conducted a meta-data review of approximately ninety-two studies since 1979 on the topic of health and marriage. Chris M. Wilson and Andrew J. Oswald. "How Does Marriage Affect Physical and Psychological Health? A Survey of the Longitudinal Evidence" IZA Discussion Paper No. 119 (June 2005). Available at SSRN: http://ssrn.com/abstract=735205.

20   R. B. Miller, C.S. Hollist, J. Olsen, and D. Law. "Marital Quality and Health Over 20 Years: A Growth Curve Analysis." Journal of Marriage and Family, 75 (2013): 667–680. doi: 10.1111/jomf.12025.

clearly shown that human intelligence exists and thrives *because* of feelings, not in spite of them. Feelings are the easiest to influence, adapt, and shape in the context of a secure relationship. We now have the science and research to promote therapies that are nurturing and that foster creativity. The three brands of therapy that are outlined in Chapters 4 through 6 represent some of the most carefully studied and effective kinds of attachment-based couples therapy available today.

THE FUNDAMENTALS OF ATTACHMENT-BASED COUPLES THERAPIES

You may be wondering how an elusive thing like emotion can be harnessed to achieve practical, measurable success in couples therapy. First, your therapist is likely to teach you how to monitor your own emotions and how to sense emotional changes in others. You'll be able to recognize what your partner is feeling, which gives you the power to choose the way you respond. By managing your own emotions, you can learn to successfully influence the emotions of your partner, even if your current circumstances make it feel impossible to imagine this.[21] There are five key areas on which attachment-based couples therapy tends to focus:

---

21   There are some circumstances where trying to rehab your relationship is contra-indicated, meaning that it could backfire and make things *worse*. Variables include 1) the skill and commitment of the therapist helping you, 2) the degree of untreated symptoms of psychological trauma (which may include mental illness or substance abuse), and 3) how much time and resources you and your partner have to apply to working with a treatment *team* (that is, more than one therapist at the same time).

1. Giving you the ability to deal constructively with your own negative emotions.

Attachment-based therapy helps you to realize that "negative" emotions such as fear, shame, anger, or jealousy are happening for a reason. They're valuable indicators of a deeper problem, despite their reputation for being overwhelming or dangerous when expressed casually in a relationship. You'll get help stabilizing these emotions while addressing their "fuel sources," the underlying emotional hurt or insecurity you have that needs more attention. No one looks forward to dredging up their own emotional baggage or working on strengthening their emotional core. It's so much easier to blame a partner for negative feelings. But if you can trust your therapist to help you do a "you-turn" and focus on correcting your reactions instead of your partner's, it truly works. By learning how to pay more attention compassionately to your own needs, overwhelming negative feelings tend to shrink and become less problematic. This allows you to communicate more clearly with your partner—without triggering his or her negative emotions, either.

2. Giving you the ability to read emotional cues more accurately.

When you're emotionally out-of-tune with your partner, you make assumptions about him or her that aren't totally accurate. Over time, each of you subconsciously begins to conform to those assumptions. When your wife says, "I need you to be around more," she may be expecting you to withdraw more or be defensive, so she may amplify her emotion to try to get through to you. You're expecting her to exaggerate her feelings so you don't pay full attention to her body language—you only notice what you're expecting to notice. It becomes a vicious cycle of disconnection. Attachment-based therapies can improve this inefficient way of communicating by instructing you on how to notice subtle emotional signals you each send with your body language. For example, you might think your wife is nagging you to spend more time with her because her expectations are too high. There may be some truth to this—that she does ask for more than she really needs—but it could also be because you've habitually given her less than she needs. That's how the pattern of her nagging you and your ignoring her has evolved. With the help of an attachment-based couples therapist, you'd be more able to respond to what she's feeling "behind" the nagging—perhaps she simply feels lonely. If you only react to the irritating nagging, you miss a critical opportunity to bond with her on a much deeper, safer, and emotionally vulnerable level. As your therapist helps you notice the loneliness, something you can relate to much more easily than nagging, you gain a powerful ability to short-circuit the toxic cycle you're in.

3. Giving you the ability to build shared meaning together and be a source of comfort.

When you and your partner first got together, you opened your lives and began to share activities that were important to you and that would help you form a history together. Perhaps you went to plays, movies, or concerts; engaged in athletic activities; or attended religious services or observed certain holidays. These rituals and routines are loaded with meaning and provide an opportunity to share yourself with your partner in a powerful way. If your relationship is distressed, the routines that once united you might now seem stale or burdensome. You may need to discuss how to modify the roles you share in these activities so that you can both feel more "at home" in your daily life together. It takes courage to have these conversations and to dream together without becoming critical or fearful about changing too much or too little. Attachment-based couples therapy can help you and your partner learn how to take small steps, together, to adjust your routines and traditions.

4. Giving you the ability to ask for what you need without putting your partner down.

Research shows that people tend to ignore their own mistakes, but to focus intently on the mistakes their relationship partner makes. Being dogmatically critical and unable to acknowledge your own mistakes is one of the clearest predictors of the dissolution of relationships. Successful partners avoid this common trap by allowing their partner to have a valid point of view that's different from theirs—they acknowledge that a difference does not mean they are categorically wrong.

Attachment-based couples therapy teaches you how to value and stand up for your own beliefs and feelings while also maintaining curiosity about your partner's beliefs and feelings. You learn that you can get more respect and care from your partner by demonstrating a consistent ability to avoid blame or judgment. By not resorting to criticism as a way of getting respect, you're saying, "I'm here for you and will meet you halfway. Are you there for me? Can you meet me halfway?"

5. You will learn to speak from the heart about what's at stake.[22]

During attachment-based couples therapy, you can expect the therapist to actively help you interrupt your arguments and shift your focus to more productive areas. They'll show you how to decode what the disagreement initially seems to be about so that you identify what deeper significance might lie beneath the words that actually emerge. Couples who aren't able to recognize deeper significance in what seem like superficial arguments end up arguing about those surface things only, leaving the most important issues unaddressed.

Speaking from the heart means sharing your own vulnerability in the relationship. For example, perhaps your parents didn't maintain a close relationship with their siblings. As a result, you missed out on getting to know your aunts, uncles, and cousins. So when your husband plans another business trip during a time you could all be with your family, you might not simply be upset about his travel plans. A part of you is subconsciously reacting to sources of emotional pain in other areas of your life—perhaps disappointment in your own career or unresolved emotional injuries from childhood.

---

22   I owe credit to Brent Atkinson for points #4 and #5.

Attachment-based couples therapy would teach you to share how your reaction about the business trip is emotionally connected to your subconscious and unspoken needs and fears. By focusing on your heart (that is, the softer side of you that's more innocent, not demanding, and is connected to your deepest hopes and wishes), it's easier for your partner to extend his heart and his genuine interest to you in turn.

SAVING JACK AND IRENE WITH ATTACHMENT THERAPY

Let's return to Jack and Irene, whom we met in the last chapter. When Jack called me to see if I could fit him into my schedule, he sounded like a man on a mission. "We got this thing happening with our couple's therapist that isn't working," he said pointedly. One of Jack's golfing buddies had shared how he and his wife were also going through a rough patch, and volunteered that they were doing couples therapy with me—and that it seemed to be helping. Jack told his friend about working with Robert, their previous therapist, and his friend could tell that my method was very different. Jack was intrigued and gave me a call.

During our first meeting, I told Jack that I'd like to see him and Irene together in every session. Irene doubted attending every session together was a good idea, given that their previous therapist had tried working with them together and had then suggested individual sessions. "Well," I replied, "let's try it together. I'll let you know if I want to meet privately with you, but I usually only do that for a brief time—and always with the goal of getting back to mutual sessions as soon as possible."

Immediately, I could see why the previous therapist had abandoned conjoint meetings. The pair was locked in a powerful tug-of-war. Irene did most of the talking and easily expressed—and demonstrated—how hot and cold her moods could run. Jack explained his thoughts about their relationship with no emotion whatsoever—it was like he was reading a parts inventory list at an automotive store.

I wanted to show Jack and Irene how my plan could help them with their situation, not just educate them about it in an abstract way. The new science of the brain tells us that feelings don't listen to logic anyway—rational thought, paradoxically, originates in feelings. By letting myself feel some of the same feelings they were feeling—relying on my limbic system's emotional attachment center—I overlaid their emotions on my own detailed emotional map. Doing this allowed me to infer what move should come next very quickly. Their pattern of either attacking or avoiding each other left them in a syncopated, empty existence. Once I could feel the same emotions they were feeling—no explanatory worksheets or exercises required—I knew which strings to tug on and which to leave alone. I relied on the clarity and hope that came from my own emotional learning about how to find a way through such a tangle.[23]

When I first met Irene, it quickly became clear that whenever she felt lonely she would lash out at Jack for not spending

---

23 This is why it's always been so critical for me to seek my own professional help individually and with my wife when our marriage has needed support.

enough time with her instead of reaching toward him and asking directly for comfort. She didn't expect that he would be there for her, so she reacted defensively. Her quickly shifting moods might appear to fit the definition of a bipolar mood swing, but *relative to Jack* she wasn't bipolar at all. Irene vacillated back and forth between her low periods and her highs in no small part because she was attached to Jack's emotional pattern of unpredictably withdrawing and seeking attention.

Jack, meanwhile, was so withdrawn that he appeared depressed. But with my help (again, sensing things in myself as I sat with Jack that he wasn't able to feel), Jack learned to tune in to a variety of emotional changes inside him. Using myself as an emotional surrogate, I stayed attuned to Jack and Irene the way a mother is attuned to her infant—I could feel what they were feeling at the same time or even slightly before they felt it.

We worked on a complaint Irene had about Jack: "I can't trust him anymore. He says one thing but does another. I don't know whether he's coming or going." I heard her criticism and tried to feel its harshness the way Jack would feel it. But I also felt more than a complaint coming from Irene. I could feel that underneath her complaint was really an emotion—vulnerability—that needed careful attention.

I told her, "It sounds like that would be really hard on you, Irene. You can't tell if Jack's really there for you. That must feel awfully lonely—"

"It's not lonely," Irene interrupted. "It's despicable behavior on his part." To me, it was clear that she was attempting to turn my attention away from her and onto Jack again.

Like most couples who have little attachment trust with each other, they learn to avoid their own vulnerabilities and instead shift attention to negativity and blame toward the other person. For example, rather than saying something vulnerable such as, "I need you. You're important to me and it hurts to not have you with me," Irene might deflect her fear of being alone by saying, "You're so selfish! Where *were* you when I needed you? All you do is think of yourself."

"Ok, I get it," I said to Irene. "You really can't stand what Jack's doing." I was being careful not to repeat her comment about Jack's behavior. I would get to that when it was time to talk to Jack. "Irene," I said, "I'm curious, though, about what *you* go through when you can't count on Jack being there for you."

Rather than using logic or my authority as the expert to convince her that we shouldn't focus on Jack, or that we could change her thoughts about the situation—which is a rational/cognitive strategy—I expressed warmth and interest about her. Specifically, I wanted to know about her feelings of despair, loneliness, and abandonment. Like some people first introduced to attachment-based therapy, Irene was skeptical. She wasn't ready to acknowledge that she had any vulnerable feelings toward Jack at all. For example, if I said, "Geez, you must feel so hurt that you have to yell at Jack to get through to him," she'd say, "I'm not hurt. I'm pissed."

Anger usually masks pain. It feels more comfortable to express our anger, or to justify ourselves with intellectual arguments than it does to lay open our neediness, emptiness, and hurt. Irene expressed skepticism about focusing on her softer feelings, so I took on the role of feeling and expressing her hurt for her. "Ouch," I'd say after she spoke angrily to Jack, "I can hear your anger and wonder if you can feel what I'm feeling. It's as if you're saying, 'I'm in so much pain I can't take this anymore and it comes out as anger, because there doesn't seem to be any other way to express it.' You're feeling desperate to get through to him…it's got to feel lonely. Can you feel that? Do you feel loneliness mixed in with your anger?"

The first few times I'd offer this type of interpretation to Irene, she'd tell me she was confused. "I have no idea what you mean," she'd say, seeming irritated with me. I knew from experience that I was on the right track, but her confusion was a sign that I needed to introduce her to this type of therapy slowly—she needed to trust me before she could open up. She needed to know that I would also focus on Jack just as much, and reveal his vulnerability too, so she didn't feel under personal attack. Even though she couldn't yet make a direct connection between her anger and her loneliness, like a detective I could see the clues. For example, after a number of sessions, she said she wished she could let her guard down more. She felt exhausted. I told her that if she could take one step toward trusting me and could let herself feel more vulnerable, it could unlock the door to feeling—and being—more cared for by Jack.

"After all," I told her after talking in-depth with Jack about his avoidance and depression, "Jack may seem hard to 'read 'and figure out, but he has feelings that work the same as yours. He wants a partner, too. It's just that he probably doesn't want to feel ashamed or outmatched when he's around you, especially in therapy. He wants the real, vulnerable Irene, not the part of you that's trying to control and limit your risk in this relationship."

It took several more sessions for Irene to understand what I was saying, let go more, and trust me so she could be more vulnerable around Jack. I also had to broaden my search for prompts that could jog Irene's memory about how to be vulnerable. In many cases, we simply can't feel vulnerable in the present moment. Subconsciously, our limbic system shuts down painful memory networks that store information about something difficult we went through in the past. From Irene's conscious perspective, her problems started and ended with Jack. But gradually she let me unlock the deeper, subconscious reason behind why she couldn't let her guard down around him. I asked her to share about what her life was like growing up when, or if, she didn't take initiative to be so direct with others about what she needed. Irene rolled her eyes.

"Are you kidding me?" she began. "*That* never happened."

"Really?" I persisted.

"I *always* had to tell my parents what I wanted. They could never seem to figure it out without me telling them, so I learned I couldn't really trust them with my real feelings. Don't get me wrong. My dad was great to me. He probably spoiled me rotten. But he and mom always had some drama... they were always preoccupied with their own battles. He was a serial cheater. He cheated on my mom—I lost track of how many times. And it consumed her, just sucked the life out of her. She was an amazing mother in spite of all of that, but geez, you know…"

"You kind of had to take care of yourself," I guessed.

Irene nodded her head in agreement. She had slowed down enough to let me become curious about some of the most unguarded moments in her life. She was letting us in "behind the scenes" of her default reaction to be self-sufficient and in control.

"It got so old dealing with all that drama. My dad, he always said he prized me and would never leave me or my mom, but I would hear about or meet these other women and it felt—it felt so awful."

"Do we have to talk about this?" Irene suddenly blurted, to stop the cascade of tender emotions that were piling up as she recalled her youth.

I looked at Jack. Prior to this, he had been gazing anywhere except at Irene. He was looking at her now like she was made out of diamonds.

"Jack," I asked, "How do you feel when you hear Irene go down this road?"

"I don't know what to say," he started, "I've never seen her like this."

"You mean this is okay for you? You're interested in what she's sharing?"

Jack's spellbound look already told me that his limbic attachment response had come to life. He was alert and calm, like someone had just handed him a sleeping baby to hold.

"Yeah, I'm good," said Jack. But I wasn't sure what "I'm good" meant. His staccato, matter-of-fact verbal reply didn't match the awestruck softness that had been pouring out of his eyes a moment before. More important, his terse answer, I knew, wasn't going to pass muster for Irene. In fact, the voice

I heard belonged to the guy reciting the auto-parts inventory. He was dutifully doing his job. That's fine for an employee, but not for a husband. Irene was craving more. She had just let us see a wounded part of herself.

I didn't want to rely on a formula about how to shape Jack's behavior into what Irene needed at this moment. Giving any sort of how-to directives would trample the budding, raw, connective emotion that was on the verge of flowing. My own gut, my limbic sense, was acting like a vulnerability antenna. There was critical attachment information being transmitted between the couple. I asked Jack if I could help him use his whole person, including his powerful emotions, to show Irene how she was impacting him when she talked about her disappointment with her dad's infidelity.

Leaning in closer to Jack, I told him I saw a light in his eyes. "What was that?" I wondered aloud.

"Well, I don't know," he began hesitantly. Then I saw the faintest hint of a smile of recognition. "I'm sorry to say my mind kind of wandered…"

"To what?" I implored, sensing very much that his "wandering" was a sign that his emotional state had shifted in a way that could truly help Irene.

"I couldn't help it, but I couldn't stop thinking about my own mom. She died when I was ten and we were left…"His voice trailed off as he looked up at me as if to ask if it was okay to not finish the sentence.

"Wow," I said. "Your mom was gone and you were just a kid. Hearing Irene open herself up took you right to that moment when she left?"

"Yeah," he said, choking up, speechless.

Tears also welled up in my own eyes. I didn't try to hide it. I knew at this point that if Jack and Irene saw my emotion it would send a subtle yet powerful signal to a part of their brains, helping them more easily expression their own "mirror" emotion (see the chapter four section on mirror neurons.)

"Jack," I said, "tell me what's it's like to know that Irene, just by being in the same room with you and opening up, can touch you like that. After all these years, she touches a new spot inside of you that helps you remember your mom?"

Jack let out a growly whine like he was being woken early from a hibernation of six months in the arctic wilderness. "Agrrraaaagh...I don't know."

"Stay with your feeling Jack, let it speak to you" I coached, knowing that his lack of words was par for the course. It's not unusual for people to have trouble articulating these types of feelings; much of the attachment mechanism of our limbic system is nonverbal.

"Sure," he said, relaxing. He was grateful I was encouraging him to take his time before speaking. I clearly wasn't going to let Irene pounce on him for not knowing how to share his deep feelings, even if they weren't consciously connected to his ability to speak.

First, for Irene's sake, to show her she could trust Jack's motives for advancing out from behind his "auto-parts" monotone, I asked him if he felt closer to Irene now than when we had first started therapy. He nodded his head many times. Then I asked him if he could to move closer to Irene on the couch—close enough so she could feel his body heat. Irene was on board. "Jack," I said, "tell Irene, 'I feel closer to you when you tell me about your dad. I want to feel this way more around you.'"

Jack easily spoke the words, because they were a true match for how he was feeling inside. He wasn't just going through the motions of being in therapy, and his ability to say those phrases made that clear to Irene. For just a second, the diamonds were back in his eyes. This time, Irene didn't miss seeing them.

"Irene, how are you doing?" I asked her. "How does it feel to hear Jack say this?"

"Different."

"Different 'good' or different, like, 'make it stop' different?"

"Definitely good. I'm not clenching my fists anymore."

"I noticed," I said. Indeed, Irene suddenly looked more relaxed from head to toe. They both looked like someone had just released them from being tied to their chairs. Even this short interaction helped them to loosen up around each other. We extended our conversation to focusing on feelings—in particular feelings of vulnerability and the memories associated with them—off and on for the next ten sessions. We focused on practical items as well, like communication skills and creating daily routines that would include the other partner. But Jack and Irene needed more than these "standard" couples therapy interventions.

Our focus on emotions was not to make Jack and Irene dwell on "downer" feelings, but to fire up their brains' natural ability to reach out to each other. There were constant challenges, which is normal. At times, each of them expressed doubts that anything productive was happening—we weren't analytically slicing and dicing the rightness or wrongness of their points of view or actions, so it was difficult to point to any "measurable" outcomes. But in each session I'd ask them to pay attention not to who was winning or scoring the best "points," but to whether they felt closer. Cautiously at first, then gratefully as the therapy progressed, they both admitted they were feeling warmer around each other. The need to be right all the time dissipated like a dense fog lifting.

WHAT BRAND IS YOUR THERAPY? THE "BIG THREE" AND WHY BRAND MATTERS

If you've ever redecorated your house or apartment, you've probably turned to national brands to guide your shopping. When you undertake home improvement projects, rather than walking into your local mom-and-pop store and limiting your choices to what happens to be in stock, you may hop onto a big-box-store website like Home Depot or Target and research all the options available in the marketplace. In the end, you might shop from the big brand or you might still end up buying from the local, independent retailer, but you used the name recognition and widespread availability of the big brands as a benchmark to guide your decision about the best buy. You can use this same principle to your advantage if you're shopping for couples therapy.

Before writing this book, I searched high and low for any published material describing what to expect when you're sitting inside the office of a couples therapist. Aside from a few pages of online advice or books written just for therapists, I couldn't find anything comprehensive. There's no big-box retail store or one-stop-shopping site where you can learn about all of the major "brands" of therapy. If only it were that easy. But especially since I've walked in your shoes, seeking a therapist for my own marriage, I can tell you about the obstacles you'll be likely to face in trying to identify the best therapist for you and how to work around them. We'll start with what makes it hard to search for a therapist:

- Training for therapists varies widely. The largest international study of psychotherapists found an astonishing 70% of psychotherapists treat couples despite the fact that couples therapy training is scarce in most graduate programs that train therapists.[24]

- Most psychotherapists operate independent of one another.

- There's no universal agreement among therapists about what kind of therapy is the best "match" for certain types of problems.

- Psychotherapists don't usually practice only one type

---

24   Orlinsky & Ronnestad, 2005. Other researchers have commented on the shocking discrepancy between therapists trained in couples therapy and the number of therapists that offer couples therapy. One study notes, "In fact, the lack of couple therapy training may account for why, although couple therapy is highly effective when studied, couple therapy is among the lowest rated for consumer satisfaction in the *Consumer Reports* study of psychotherapies (Seligman, 1995), which did not control for therapist training" (Lebow, J. L., Chambers, A. L., Christensen, A. and Johnson, S. M. (2012), Research on the Treatment of Couple Distress. *Journal of Marital and Family Therapy*, 38: 145–168. doi: 10.1111/j.1752-0606.2011.00249.x)

of therapy. Many consider themselves "eclectic," a term that means they draw upon many traditions of therapy in any given session and aren't defined by a single philosophy.

If these sound like daunting uncertainties, don't despair. There's hope. This book was written to make it easier to navigate these very obstacles. There are many effective styles of couples therapy out there—too many to review all of them in this book. One type of couples therapy, attachment-based couples therapy, is quickly becoming the most highly regarded type of therapy among experienced couples therapists. Among therapies that include attachment-based concepts, I will discuss the three most predominant, which I refer to as The Big Three. The Big Three consist of: Imago Relationship Therapy, Gottman Method Couples Therapy, and Emotionally Focused Therapy for Couples. These therapies have several things in common that distinguish them from other types of therapy, such as:

- Widespread recognition of methods—thousands of therapists have been trained in each of these three methods in every US state and in many parts of the world.

- Therapists practicing these therapies must complete a rigorous certification program that includes one-on-one review of video-recorded work of the therapist with actual clients.[25] Each has organizational

---

25   Some training programs for couples therapists allow therapists to do training online or at home, without personal observation or supervision before issuing a certificate.

infrastructure that is over ten years old and supports research, therapist training workshops, annual conferences, professional publications, and local collaboration with other therapists.

- You can walk into any major bookstore and find more than one bestselling book based on concepts from these three brands of therapy. It is also usually easy to find public workshops led by a certified presenter in most states that is based on the books.

Each of these brands draws on the same general principles of attachment theory. However, each operates at a slightly different frequency, ranging from "touchy feely" to more intellectual or skill-based. Once you determine which brand is the best fit for you, however, you'll still find some variations among how they're employed by therapists. If one brand, as it's delivered by a certain therapist, seems to fall short of what you need, it's critical that you don't give up. Find the one that is the best fit for your style, and then find a therapist who can deliver that style.[26] Attachment therapy is highly personal. Because it's related to your formative years and individual development, the right therapist can tailor your experience to you and your spouse.

Take heart: the fact that you've decided to pursue therapy together has already attached you to one another in more ways and more deeply than you can imagine.

---

26   A properly trained and experienced attachment-based therapist uses attachment techniques only when appropriate. There are circumstances in which attachment-based couples therapy is *not* recommended initially, such as in abusive or highly reactive relationships.

PART II.
RECOMMENDED TOOLS

CHAPTER 4

IMAGO RELATIONSHIP THERAPY

"Your partner is not a facsimile of you."

—Harville Hendrix,
co-creator of Imago Relationship Therapy

I MAGO RELATIONSHIP THERAPY (pronounced "ih-mah-goh") is an attachment-based couples therapy known for helping couples improve communication and connection. There's a wide variation in practice style among therapists who advertise as Imago therapists, but these key features provide a snapshot of the Imago approach to couples therapy:

- Imago has a structured format. It's focused on learning communication skills and engaging in exercises designed to help you reduce conflict and grow closer as a couple.

- The therapy focuses on how your past relationship experiences have influenced your choice of a partner and it gives you a way to understand each other's needs and to approach each other with compassion and empathy.

- You may be asked to do some out-of-session homework to complete either on your own or with your partner.

If these aspects of Imago Relationship Therapy sound valuable to you, read on for more detail.

BAGGAGE CLAIM: FIND THE HIDDEN PURPOSE OF YOUR RELATIONSHIP

"Stop acting like my mother." This is a common complaint overheard by couples therapists every day. Have you ever wondered why some of the same scenes from your parents' relationship show up in your own? Or why "old baggage" from previous relationships interferes with the relationship you're in now? Imago Relationship Therapy is designed specifically to help you "check your baggage," so that your past no longer interferes with the enjoyment of a vibrant relationship with the person you're with today.

Imago Relationship Therapy is based on the book *Getting the Love You Want* by Harville Hendrix and his wife, Helen LaKelly Hunt. First published in 1988, the book quickly became a bestseller and has remained one ever since. *Getting the Love You Want* has inspired a generation of couples to uncover the subconscious reasons they were attracted to each other in the first place. Using their therapist's guidance, they figure out how their present conflict is linked to old, subconscious patterns from their past. They use this information to end counterproductive hostility toward each other, make improvements in their relationship that can be life-changing, and forge a new kind of "conscious" partnership.

MARRIAGE AS THERAPY: WHY PAY A THERAPIST TO DO A JOB YOUR PARTNER CAN LEARN?

For decades, Freud and his many followers believed that therapy patients reverted to behaviors learned in childhood when it came to dealing with their own feelings toward the therapist. It was the therapist's job to point out these behaviors and to catalyze a struggle of will that ultimately forced the patient to change old behaviors and prove the therapist wrong.[27] For example, if you felt that your therapist was acting cold toward you, he'd point out that it must be your subconscious tendency to expect him to act that way, because of the way you experienced your parents as a child. You'd usually spend years in therapy, learning to clarify such assumptions and replacing your automatic reactions with nuanced insight from the therapist. When it came to couples in therapy, however, Hendrix

---

27   Many modern psychoanalysts today, trained with relationship-building skills, may not be nearly as confrontational as early analysts, but the legacy of Freud casts a long shadow and his theories still play a large part in the classical training of many therapists and psychiatrists.

coined the phrase "marriage as therapy." He believed in a different dynamic. He believed that an intimate relationship between two romantic partners was ultimately where power struggles were most plentiful, and, therefore, it would be far more efficient to tinker therapeutically with feelings you have toward your partner than to focus on your feelings toward the therapist. After all, you can't take your therapist home with you. But if you and your partner both learn how to create the healing effects of therapy on your own, then you could get more accomplished with standard psychoanalysis.

CONSCIOUS PARTNERSHIP: WHEN IT'S SAFE ENOUGH TO BE YOURSELF

The Imago philosophy is based on the idea that all romantic relationships go through predictable stages. Infatuation and romantic feelings eventually give way to the inevitable power struggles that occur when you realize your partner is not a carbon copy of you. During this first stage—the romantic phase—couples become close and are flexible and forgiving. But during the second stage—the power struggle phase—couples grow apart and can become inflexible and negative toward each other. The goal of Imago therapy is to reverse the power struggle phase and create a third, new phase defined by trust and consideration of the other. This phase is called a *conscious partnership*.

In a conscious partnership, couples actively interrupt patterns of negativity and avoidance of intimacy. You each take responsibility for creating habits that are safe and respectful of each other's feelings. When safety and respect figure strongly in your relationship, each of you can let your guard down and become more open to changes that occur naturally in the course of a long relationship. You can be yourself and still be considerate of your partner. You actively try to show each other more vulnerability—for example, sharing your needs in a nondemanding way—and you attempt to teach your partner how to specifically meet these needs in a way that respects his or her limitations.[28]

WHAT TO EXPECT WHEN WORKING WITH AN IMAGO RELATIONSHIP THERAPIST

"Imago" is the Latin word for *image*. Imago therapy is based upon the theory that we perceive our partner not as he or she really is, but filtered through the subconscious lens of formative experiences we had growing up. For example, you may think of your husband as socially energetic or always the life of the party, and this can cause tension between you because perhaps you prefer to be reserved. You complain to him about his behavior, but, from your perspective, he doesn't really make substantial changes. He even takes the opposite position: he might think that you're too sensitive to his big personality because you're so withdrawn. Neither one of you can get through to the other.

---

28   Hendrix developed Imago therapy to counter what he saw as a problem with the dominant thinking in psychology, namely that problems in relationships are made worse by treating the two partners individually, instead of as a couple. He thought that psychotherapists were too quick to diagnose the symptoms of individual mental health issues, such as depression or bipolar disorder, while ignoring how these symptoms can *be caused or cured* by the relationship.

Stalemate. Imago theory asserts that, while you both legitimately have some real differences, your associations from experiences you had in prior relationships (especially painful memories) color your current experiences and interfere with your ability to see personality differences accurately.

By sifting through key moments in your past relationships, an Imago therapist helps you put your partner's behavior into perspective. Continuing with the same example above, you might associate your father's gregariousness with a tendency for infidelity and ultimately the demise of your parents' marriage. Although you've put their divorce behind you, it made a painful impression on you for much of your youth. Now, whenever your husband really enjoys himself and is playful with other people instead of paying attention to you, your mind and body subconsciously re-create the discomfort you felt as a kid. You feel a visceral change in your body, an unstoppable emotional reaction—one that you've probably unthinkingly experienced many times earlier in your life. In Imago therapy, you'll be taught to recognize when your emotions are being "hijacked" by subconscious connections to your past.

Your therapist will also teach you to present your feelings in such a way that helps you successfully connect to—instead of alienate—your partner. For example, before Imago therapy you might commonly express your feelings with a complaint: "You know I really hate it when you've been drinking and start showing off. Can't you knock it off?" After Imago therapy, you'd have practice transforming a complaint into a productive request: "I get nervous at parties as it is, but especially when you're paying attention to other people. I got teased a lot as a kid in social situations, and I'd feel a lot better if you were by my side a few times tonight. Could we spend some of our time there together before you go off with your friends?"

When conflict persists, many couples draw the conclusion that they've married the wrong person. Imago therapists tend to emphasize that relationship differences aren't a sign of a bad relationship. They view conflict as a sign that the couple just hasn't figured out the hidden meaning of their relationship. The Imago philosophy is that conflict exists to help each partner mature as a person. To be free of conflict, one must accept the aspects of the other that are hardest to like. For example, when my wife and I participated in Imago therapy, we appreciated learning how we each fit into the other's relationship history. Discovering how we could take on new roles, such as the role of a healer of past injuries, helped us rise above complaining about day-to-day irritations. The power struggle about who's right or who gets their way was replaced by a higher calling: to act with awareness. We acknowledge that we come from different places, each with our own values. Now when we disagree, it doesn't feel threatening. We have a tacit agreement that we're always on the same team, united even through differences of opinion. Being more flexible makes our lives fit together much better.

KEY TOOLS IN IMAGO RELATIONSHIP THERAPY

The primary area of focus in Imago is communication between partners. How many times have you said to your partner, "Are you even hearing what I'm saying?" Research shows that poor communication is one of the most consistent causes of frustration with couples considering therapy. Pick up any relationship book or browse the Internet for information about relationship problems, and you'll likely see this idea repeated: communication is key. Nearly all types of couples therapies offered today include communication tools in their bag of tricks.

Imago works especially with communication to both diagnose and to cure a couple's attachment problems. This is the key difference between Imago and other types of therapy, including the other two attachment-based therapies discussed in this section, Gottman Method Couples Counseling and Emotionally Focused Therapy for couples. Once you've read each of the three chapters that cover these three couples therapies, you should have an idea of which method is the best fit for you and your partner—or you may find a therapist who integrates some or all of them, in addition to other useful approaches.

The primary exercise that couples are exposed to in Imago is called "Intentional Couple's Dialogue." If you choose to work with an Imago couples therapist, you can expect that you'll be exposed to this method early and often. To someone unfamiliar with the progression of Imago therapy, the Intentional Couple's Dialogue appears to be just a simplistic mimicking game. But don't underestimate the benefit of Intentional Dialogue. For those patient enough to use it to its full extent, the results are surprisingly powerful.

In Intentional Couple's Dialogue, one partner talks (the *sender*) while the other partner listens (the *receiver*). The sender sends a short message: "I'm upset that you forgot to stop at the grocery store." The receiver repeats the message but doesn't paraphrase. The sender's exact words are used as much as possible: "You said that you're upset that I forgot to stop at the grocery store."

As the receiver in Imago's Intentional Couple's Dialogue,[29] you're not allowed to ask questions or to add your own thoughts to the phrase. Intentional Dialogue is all about giving the sender the experience that he or she is free from your mental filter, which changes and interprets the words and meaning of what you hear. Your job is to hear your partner's message—not the way that you may want to hear it so that it suits your own needs or understanding, but the way your partner *feels* it.

TINA AND SAL TRY TO MAKE IT WORK USING IMAGO THERAPY

Tina met Sal in college. Mutual friends introduced them to each other at a party and they "hung out" for a few months before things quickly grew serious. After they graduated they dated for two more years, then married the week after Sal's

---

29   Some of you may recognize Imago dialogue as a form of active listening. Active listening isn't native only to Imago. Many other psychotherapy approaches use it, and some Fortune 500 companies even teach a simplified version to customer service employees, simply because poor communication costs companies money. However, the form of active listening in Imago has several key distinctions that make it more complex. Instead of just being a passive and head-nodding listener, active listening—Imago style—requires the listener to interrupt the sender to confirm that the message is being received correctly.

twenty-fourth birthday. A year later, when Tina became pregnant, her college friends were the first to notice that Tina and Sal's normally quick-witted banter had become laced with pointedly hurtful barbs and jabs.

When Tina first met Sal, he made her feel special. He was amused by her talkativeness, possibly because his family was very reserved and anything but talkative. "Growing up, my family dinners were often silent," Sal told his therapist. "We could go an entire week without talking during dinner!" Sal's mom always claimed to "have the blues" and probably drank too much. His dad was stoic and never let his feelings show when he was around. Three-quarters of the time, he wasn't. When they were dating, Sal considered Tina's loquaciousness to be incredibly novel, almost magical. But over time, familiarity bred contempt. Tina confessed she didn't have an "off switch." Instead of Sal responding to her and coming out of his shell, he retreated further and further into the silence he was used to when he was growing up. The more Tina talked, the more Sal tuned her out. The more Sal tuned her out, the more pressured Tina felt, which caused her to talk more. Their pursue-withdraw communication style led to huge fights that both accused the other of starting. Neither one would back down. Things weren't going to get better unless they got help.

When Sal and Tina started Imago Therapy, they immediately appreciated how their therapist, Jen, helped them slow down and really listen to each other.

"I know the way I badger him when he's shutting me out is counterproductive," Tina admitted, "and I know it doesn't do any good to call him names. But we can both really get carried away. All the while I'm thinking, 'What are we even fighting about'?"

Jen asked Sal and Tina to try a new way of talking to each other, one that was more structured than they were used to. The look on Sal's face seemed to indicate that he was ready for anything other than what he was dealing with then. But Tina had some questions.

"What do you mean by 'structured'?" she asked. "Is it structured as in we write down what we are thinking or something?" Tina's way of dealing with her anxiety in a new situation was to ask a lot of questions—it helped her think everything through. Sal was just the opposite. He liked to let things unfold a while before saying anything or attempting to figure them out.

"Well," said Jen, "if it's okay with you, I'd like to show you what I mean for about ten minutes. Then we can stop to talk about how it's going. Does that sound good?"

Tina was able to participate in the exercise without anxiety after she was satisfied that Jen would leave time in the session for her to process her reaction.

Jen explained to Sal and Tina that each would take turns being the sender, while the other repeated only the words that were said. Then the receiver was to ask, "Did I get you?" followed by, "Is there more?"

Jen helped Sal find a "safe" topic, one that wouldn't ignite an argument. They chose his dad's upcoming retirement.

"Ok, Tina, are you available now to have a dialogue about my dad's retirement?" started Sal.

Tina grinned from ear to ear. The idea that Sal was

approaching *her*, spelling out in detail what he wanted to talk about regarding his dad's retirement, made her laugh.

"What's so funny?" Sal asked, a grin also appearing across his face.

"Never mind," she said. "I'm just enjoying this."

"Ok," Sal chuckled, half nervous and half enjoying himself too.

"So my dad's retiring, and there's going to be a big thing for him down on the river."

Jen jumped in. "Ok, Tina, can you mirror this back to Sal and capture his words? Repeat his words," she instructed.

"Sure," began Tina. "The shop's going to have your dad's party at the Jefferson Club, right?"

"Ask him if you got it," coached Jen. The way Tina had paraphrased Sal's words could be a stumbling block, depending on Sal's feelings about this particular topic.

"Did I get you?" asked Tina.

Jen looked to Sal and gave him further information about the exercise. "As the sender, you have the liberty to say, 'You got me,' 'That was it,' or 'Not quite it. What I said was…' And then you repeat what you wanted her to hear."

"Well, actually, what I said was that my dad's retirement is coming up and there's going to be a big thing down at the river," corrected Sal.

This time Tina had her instructions clear. She stuck to a nearly verbatim mirroring of Sal's words. "Did I get it?" she asked. "And is there more?"[30] "Yes, you got it. And yes, there's

---

30   In Imago dialogue, couples use the phrase "Is there more?" to help the receiver gain clarification and to reassure the sender that he or she still has the

more." Sal sang back to her, straightening his back and raising his head, almost as though he felt that he could hold his own a bit more already. Talking had always been Tina's turf. But immediately Sal could see how the structure of the Imago Dialogue was going to help him. He finally had a tool to respectfully stop Tina from finishing his sentences with her own words or change what he was saying into something that somehow related to her.

Sal continued to share details about his father's upcoming party, and Tina stopped him each time she needed to slow him down so she could mirror (repeat) his words. When he was finished, they switched roles. They both admitted to Jen that the dialogue was a very different way of talking. Although it was a lot of work to follow the rules, they both felt safer than they did during their ordinary dueling monologues. And they acknowledged that those fights resulted in neither one feeling understood.

THE TURNING POINT: TINA AND SAL FIND HIDDEN MEANING IN THEIR STRUGGLE

By their third session with Jen, Tina and Sal had already practiced the basic Couples Dialogue several times with relatively simple topics, both in sessions and a few times at home. Their therapist focused the next session on doing what's called the Caring Behaviors Exercise. During this exercise, Sal and Tina took turns talking about caring behaviors they no longer did

---

floor. Imago therapists say that the tone of voice makes all the difference. As you might imagine, to say "Is there more?" sarcastically, hoping your partner will stop talking, doesn't work too well.

("I used to enjoy giving you back rubs." "I used to call your mom and check in on her."). They then agreed to each attempt one of the old caring behaviors each week. Next, they used the dialogue process to discuss the specific points of struggle that had brought them into couples therapy. Jen advised them that she'd help the sender soften complaints, which focused too much on the other person, and instead focused their dialogue on their own unmet needs or wishes.

"We all have unmet needs that show up in our relationship as complaints or negativity, because in a very old, primitive part of our brain, an 'alarm' goes off that says 'Hey, no one's taking care of me!' When our needs aren't met, we react from a very vulnerable place. Like a baby, we sort of scream our heads off and hope someone helps us," she explained.

"As adults," Jen continued, "we revert to blaming and criticizing or withdrawing and numbing when we feel threatened. It's an infantile state. The only productive thing about being negative is that it gets attention. After you get your partner's attention, however, the negativity serves no purpose other than to send your partner into a panic or put him or her on the defensive, which only makes it harder for him or her to care for you." Her point was that when negativity is being directed at you, it's *really* hard to listen, to mirror the person's words and remain nondefensive.

"So now that you both understand how Imago dialogue slows down your conversations, you'll find it's safer to talk about things and you won't insert the negativity. I'll help you with this. When you're not negative, softer feelings like hurt or sadness or loneliness tend to surface more easily. These are much, much easier to mirror and empathize with—easier to attach to. I'm going to help you with that too."

Tina was the sender for the first dialogue that really helped Sal see her in a totally new light. She began by saying she wanted to talk about Sal's new habit of leaving the door unlocked when he came home and joined her in bed.

"You come home and act as though you live by yourself," she began, then proceeded to list all of Sal's trespasses.

Jen intervened. "Jen, tell him how you feel when you think he's acting like he lives by himself." Tina was focusing only on Sal's behavior, missing the opportunity to reveal the impact it had on her.

"Alone. Like I'm living by myself."

"Yes," Jen said, "This is good. Tell him about what that's like, to feel alone even though you're living with him."

Tina paused and looked at the floor to steady herself. It was a big shift toward vulnerability to not instinctively keep railing about Sal's behavior and instead open up more about how it made her feel.

"When you forget to lock the door, I feel so lonely. It's as if I don't even exist to you. But then I criticize you for being irresponsible because I don't want to show you how alone I feel."

Sal mirrored everything back and then tried to use an additional step in the dialogue exercise called "validation," but his own feelings of betrayal showed through. "That makes sense," said Sal. "But if that's true, I'd never know it," he snapped.

Jen cautioned Sal to remain purely in his role as receiver. "Sal, there's going to be time when we switch and get to process your feelings about what Tina's saying instead of just listening and repeating her words. Your feelings make sense, too, but can you wait until it's your turn?" Even though Jen was strict about not letting them speak unless it was their turn, Sal and Tina appreciated the predictability and safety such structure provided.

"Sal," said Jen, keeping her focus on him for a moment, "Tina's just said something she's never said to you before about her protective reaction—she jumps on you and criticizes. Can you look at her and let her know you appreciate this effort by saying, 'That makes sense. I'm really available to hear more about your fear of being alone.'"

Sal didn't find it easy to follow Jen's lead. Instead, he wanted to highlight the part about him feeling jumped on and criticized by Tina, so Jen spent the rest of the session processing that with Sal. She checked back with Sal at the start of the following session. He was in a better place, and was much more open to hearing about Tina's fear of being alone and how she protected herself by criticizing him.

Jen asked Tina to tell the story about how she'd learned to hide her fear of being alone in her childhood.[31] Tina talked about how she had two older sisters. Her parents would intervene in their spats only if there had been real bloodshed. In that environment, with little parental involvement, Tina's best weapon against her sisters was her sharp tongue. Jen helped Tina talk about the part of her that attacked Sal when she felt alone. "Tell Sal what would have happened if you'd never

---

31   Not everyone is quick to make connections between present-day habits and events in the past. This account is a condensed version of many Imago Therapy sessions, to illustrate the key points that are typically addressed in this style of therapy.

learned to be so quick to shred one of your sisters. Could you imagine that little girl [referring to Tina] without a way to stand up for herself and fight?"

"Aw, she'd be a sitting duck," Tina said with familiarity. "She'd have no one to help her."

"Right," said Jen, lowering and slowing down her voice. "She'd have no one if she didn't—" Jen stopped mid-sentence because two tears were making their way down Tina's face.

"Is this okay for you?" asked Jen. Tina agreed she was comfortable showing her vulnerable emotion, because she trusted that Sal was "on her side" at that point.

The more Tina talked about her sisters, the more interested Sal became. Jen could see a kind of protective instinct forming between Sal and Tina right before her eyes, as Tina spoke through tears that were by then flowing freely. He could see her sadness clearly for the first time. Tina continued, "There was no room to breathe, because we were so mean to each other. I always had to watch my back..." Sal continued to mirror and summarize each part of Tina's recollection, and he voiced his real empathy and concern about imagining her in that state—vulnerable and wanting support.

Jen used the Imago dialogue to delve underneath the outer layer of their struggle and into the heart of Tina's pain, which was rooted in childhood and was being reactivated by Sal's behavior. Sal was happy and relieved to witness this transformation without being blamed for Tina's pain. He told Tina how it moved him to think of her needing his protection. Sal had shared in previous sessions that when he was growing up, he hadn't had much opportunity to prove his competence to people who mattered. And because he thought Tina disapproved of him, he never thought she might be the one looking to him for comfort and protection. When given the option, and with guidance from their therapist, Sal and Tina gladly took on their new roles. They became more compassionate and less critical of each other's weaknesses. Imago therapy helped them realize that, despite outward appearances that sometimes suggested otherwise, each of them was uniquely capable of doing the very things that the other needed to feel loved.

Learning about how to use the Intentional Couple's Dialogue also gave Tina and Sal a kind of thermostat—he couldn't be passive anymore when she was talking, and she couldn't steamroll him with her words. In fact, he was surprised to find it satisfying to slow Tina down so he could repeat her words. Tina appreciated hearing herself through Sal's mirroring of her. For the first time, she realized how hard it must be for someone to understand her feelings, because she used a sheer volume of words to explain her feelings—which at the same time kept her feelings hidden.

After getting used to the unintuitive way of using Intentional Dialogue when talking with each other, each of them learned new things about feelings. This greatly improved the quality of their conversations. In the past when Tina talked a lot, Sal had assumed her openness indicated that she felt confident and in control. With time, he realized the opposite was true. She often talked a lot when she felt anxious and insecure. Knowing the reason behind Tina's need to talk so much, Sal felt safer to take a risk and say more about his feelings. He was even pleasantly surprised to find out that if he ventured to share his feelings (unsolicited by Tina), Tina became more sensitive to Sal and agreed to tone down her sarcasm when she was upset. Similarly, Tina had had no idea that Sal was hurt by the language she used because he never showed it. They were both deeply moved to think of themselves as actors who were capable of going back in time, figuratively, to replay important childhood scenes as the wiser and more compassionate figures that each needed, but hadn't quite had growing up.

WHY DID IMAGO THERAPY WORK WITH TINA AND SAL?

Imago Therapy worked with Tina and Sal because it put an end to the negative assumptions they made about each other's intent. They didn't even realize they were doing it in the first place. Imago theory calls this *unconscious communication.* They didn't have the tools needed to put aside their distorted assumptions and become genuinely interested in the perspective of the other person. Unless you train yourself to listen from the perspective of the other, you're bound to hear what he or she is saying through the same sifter through which you filter your own experiences. The experiences that Tina and Sal had early in life that were most difficult or painful had formed a mental map that filtered and distorted how each interpreted, and reacted to, the other's communication.

Tina and Sal's Imago therapist educated them about how communication happens at the pace of the slowest member, and that the slowest member is always the listener. She gave them Imago dialogue as a tool to slow down their conversations and learn to listen more carefully. This was an intellectual concept new to them both. Introducing key concepts in an educational format was the beginning stage of Imago Therapy that gave Tina and Sal a clear sense that the therapy they were getting was taking them somewhere.

MONKEY SEE, MONKEY DO: IMAGO AND MIRROR NEURONS

When we listen to someone speak, we hear sounds that our brain interprets into words. In turn, we interpret the words into meaning. This process occurs automatically and quickly. And since our brain must process the torrent of words that flow in any normal conversation, we rely on this "autopilot" feature to survive and function efficiently in the world.

Our brain doesn't really perceive reality directly.[32] That requires far too much computing power. Instead, it makes guesstimates and mental shortcuts about what reality *ought* to be, based on prior learning. Thank goodness we're able to do this. Without an ability to rapidly decode another person's speech into meaningful, truncated snippets, the act of hearing someone talk to us would be confusing, exhausting, and

---

32   There are many interesting studies that look at this phenomenon from a variety of angles. Psychologists Dennis Proffitt and Jessica Witt, at the University of Virginia, studied physical sense and sports performance, and found that physically fit people see hills as less steep than physically unfit people (2012). Baseball players who are hitting well also perceive the ball to be larger than do players who are not hitting well. Football kickers see goalposts as either narrower or wider, depending on the success of their past few kicks.

unpleasant. In fact, all of what we sense from the outside world—our sight, our taste, and our sense of touch—would be crude if not for an amazing component of our brain physiology called *mirror neurons.*

Mirror neurons were discovered in the early 1990s in research done with monkeys in Italy.[33] When primates, including humans, watch other primates doing something, special brain cells called mirror neurons light up. It turns out that mirror neurons create an internal representation of behavior we observe or hear in others, as though we're doing that behavior ourselves. Mirror neurons are a big reason we're entertained just by watching other humans and can partly explain our love as spectators of the performing arts and sports. But mirror neurons play an even bigger role in how we relate to other humans. Mirror neurons, because they fire without our control just by being in the presence of another human, are a literal, real, physiological connection to the humans around us. If you walk by someone struggling to carry a heavy package, your mirror neurons light up. If you pay close attention, you may actually feel the heaviness of the package yourself.

Before the discovery of mirror neurons, scientists generally believed that we used the rational parts of our brain to relate to others and interpret behavior. But now it's mostly agreed upon that we use feelings, not rational thought, to relate to and interpret others. Because of mirror neurons and our limbic (emotional) brain, we can simply sense the feelings of others around us. The meaning behind the faintest twitch of the

33   Di Pellegrino, G., L. Fadiga, L. Fogassi, V. Gallese, and G. Rizzolatti. *Experimental Brain Research.* 1992;91(1):1432–1106.

mouth, the raise of the eyebrow, or a roll of the eyes is almost instantly transmitted from one human to another. Thanks to mirror neurons, when one person feels tenderness, fear, or surprise, so will the person nearest to them. Most of this information is transmitted subconsciously. Put simply, feelings are contagious. Mirror neurons help us infer the meaning of other people's actions or speech, and their existence makes us feel as though what we're thinking is reality.

So when you and your partner are disagreeing with each other, how do you know if your feelings are based on what your partner is really doing or saying, or if they're based on your mirror neuron "image," which can be based more on you and your past experiences than on the present reality? The brilliance of Imago therapy is that it acts upon the latter.

Imago therapy gets you to recognize:

1. "I have an internal representation of my partner that is often heavily skewed by my past memories (my "baggage"), and…"

2. "Unless I have the means to detach from the assumptions manufactured by my own baggage, my partner will never have the chance to be or do anything other than what I expect him/her to be or do."

The second point is incredibly important. In fact, if you don't actively root out your own mental distortions of your partner, your reacting "as if" contributes significantly to way that your partner acts.

IS IMAGO OUR STYLE?

Want to know if Imago therapy is for you? Take a look at this summary of the features that differentiate Imago Relationship Therapy from other therapies. Keep in mind that some therapists use the Imago techniques all the time, while others may use them only when the techniques are the best choice. Ask your therapist how closely he or she adheres to the "pure" Imago model, if that's important to you.

Imago is unique because:

- It's typically a highly structured approach. The therapist has an agenda to teach you basic "Imago skills," which include the Intentional Couple's Dialogue communication exercise, an exploration of past relationships, and regularly sharing appreciations with each other. If you like freedom and want space to talk freely, Imago could feel too rigid. On the other hand, some couples really like the structure because it virtually guarantees that they won't be fighting during sessions.

- Imago is an attachment-based therapy. Its methods aim to improve intimacy and restore connection. Its philosophy is based on the idea that your current relationship repeats scenes from prior relationships that didn't go well for you. You can choose to intentionally redesign these scenes and create the outcome that you've always wanted.

- You may be asked to do homework and fill in written answers to questions during Imago therapy. For example, during one exercise, you create a "vision" for your relationship using positive and achievable goal-statements. During another exercise, you discuss—and ultimately try to eliminate—activities that you engage in that divert energy away from your relationship. During a third exercise that you might learn in Imago therapy, you transform frustration into what's called a *behavior change request.*

Imago is goal-directed in that it teaches the Imago communication skills of dialogue and how to understand subconscious feelings that may have roots in childhood. When following the "pure" Imago method, you're asked to set aside your need to be right and to listen to each other's feelings. You're encouraged to find ways to stay connected to your partner rather than to find a solution to your disagreements.

FITTING-ROOM QUIZ

Choose one answer to each question that best describes you to see if Imago might be a good fit for you and your partner.

A. How much do you think your relationship needs a complete communication overhaul?

1. Our communication is a train wreck—neither one of us "gets" the other.

2. We go off the rails frequently trying to communicate but sometimes get it right.

3. We communicate with respect and care but hit some rough spots every now and then.

4. We couldn't possibly communicate any better—we finish each other's sentences (and don't mind).

B. Can you follow directions even if you can't see the immediate benefit?

1. Without a doubt. I could build Noah's Ark in the Sahara Desert if you gave me the instructions.

2. I can follow the rules most of the time but occasionally wander off the path.

3. I wander off the path often but can occasionally follow the rules.

4. Definitely not. Stop signs are only suggestions to me.

C. Are you open to the idea that you and your partner are meant to be together to help each other complete unfinished emotional development from childhood?

1. Like this is news? Sign me up for *Unconscious Associations from Childhood 101*.

2. I'm a little skeptical, but I'd like to see where this could take me.

3. I'll go along for the ride, but I'm not really a fan of this idea.

4. Stop this train. I want to get off.

D. How comfortable are you with this statement: You can be right or you can be in a relationship?

1. Is a fish comfortable in the ocean? I agree with being agreeable 100 percent.

2. I'm aware that relationships are about give and take, but I need reminders sometimes.

3. Compromise feels like failure to me, but I can do it if I really need to.

4. Are you kidding me? It's my way or the highway.

E. Do you prefer a therapist who isn't ambiguous about his/her belief that even really "bad" relationships can be saved?

1. Yes. Send in the cavalry!

2. It's appealing to me to think that radical transformations happen in relationships, but I'm not always too sure.

3. I'd rather that this opinion wasn't pushed too strongly by our therapist but I understand that this may be how she defines her job.

4. Do Not Resuscitate!

How to Score Your Answers

Add the numbers you chose for your answers, and then use the chart below to determine what kind of match Imago Relationship Therapy is for you. Do the same for your partner's score, and use the fit rating to further assess your compatibility with this brand of therapy.

> **Just Right:** If your total is 5–10, it's a great fit, and you'll likely be intrigued by Imago. Strongly consider finding a therapist who uses this kind of therapy.

> **Loose Fit:** If your total is 11–15, it's a decent fit, but some aspects of Imago methods may not thrill you. You might want to look into Imago and possibly compare it with an alternative to be sure.

> **Tight Squeeze:** If your total is 16–20, you could be more annoyed by than receptive to Imago methods. Proceed with caution, and interview potential therapists carefully. Feel free to work with an Imago therapist if he or she uses Imago methods judiciously and perhaps in combination with other methods that are a better fit for you—perhaps from either Emotionally Focused Therapy or the Gottman Method Couples Therapy.

Keep in mind that this "fit-ness" test is a very rough guide. Just like clothing sizes vary between manufacturers, you could find wide variation between any two Imago therapists. Depending on the therapist's exposure to other significant couples therapy training, he or she may depend exclusively on using Imago methods or only use it only when he or she determines that it's a good fit.

FURTHER READING

Harville Hendrix, *Getting the Love You Want: A Guide for Couples* (New York: St. Martin's Press, 1988).

Harville Hendrix, *Keeping the Love You Find: A Personal Guide* (New York: Atria, 1993).

Harville Hendrix, *Receiving Love* (New York: Atria, 2004).

Harville Hendrix and H.L. Hunt, *Making Marriage Simple: Ten Truths for Changing the Relationship You Have into the One You Want* (New York: Random House, 2013).

CHAPTER 5

GOTTMAN METHOD COUPLES THERAPY

"Admit when you're wrong. Shut up when you're right."

—Dr. John Gottman

L IKE THE OTHER therapies detailed in this book, you'll find variation among therapists who practice Gottman Method Couples Therapy. Here's a snapshot of what you can usually expect during your work with most therapists trained in this approach:

- Your therapist provides clear structure and goals for your sessions based on decades of Gottman's research with couples to determine what predicts a successful relationship. For example, Gottman therapists debunk the myth that successful couples don't fight. In fact, successful couples may fight often, but they do it in a way that never compromises key aspects of the relationship.

- Gottman-trained therapists like to collect a lot of data from you. You might have to fill out questionnaires for an hour or two when you first start working with your therapist and a few more throughout the course of your sessions. Some therapists will collect live biofeedback during sessions by using a device connected to your finger that detects physiological signs of stress. You're taught how to relax during tense moments.

- You'll see exercises designed to improve how you and your partner deal with conflict as well as exercises designed to help you learn more about your partner and deepen your intimacy, emotional connection, and understanding.

If you resonate with some of these aspects of Gottman Method Couples Therapy, read on for more detail.

THE SCIENCE OF COUPLES

What would you give if you could predict whether you would be in a stable marriage, unhappily married, or divorced six years from now? John Gottman became famous in the field of marriage counseling because of his documented claim that, through research, he could do just that. Never before had someone made scientifically replicated predictions about the essential ingredients for relationship success. Gottman's decades of collecting data led him to claim that he could diagnose a relationship accurately in just fifteen minutes. This earned him a spotlight in the opening chapter of Malcolm Gladwell's popular book *Blink: The Power of Thinking without Thinking,* about how having the right data makes it possible to make snap decisions accurately. But while Gottman may have catapulted to fame because of his first-of-its kind findings about the behavior of couples, one of his most lasting influences was the creation of a unique, scientifically informed treatment for couples, the Gottman Method Couples Therapy.[34]

RESEARCH FROM THE LOVE LAB

It's impossible to talk about what you'd expect if you went into couples therapy with a therapist trained in Gottman Method Couples Therapy without touching on Gottman's research. All of it took place in what would be later dubbed the "Love Lab," a studio apartment in downtown Seattle where couples were videotaped continuously for twenty-four-hour periods. The techniques used in the Gottman Method are based upon those findings.

---

34 Two of the couples therapy methods described in this book—the Gottman Method Couples Therapy and Emotion-Focused Therapy—are both based on research. But how "research" is defined is different between the two. Gottman Method is a scientifically informed couples therapy, while Emotion-Focused Therapy (EFT) is validated by outcome research. The difference is no small source of debate within the field of couples therapy but doesn't need to be a big factor in your choice of a couples therapist. "Scientifically informed" means that the methods that Gottman designed for use in couples therapy were based on scientific research about the behavior of couples in general. Outcome research, done extensively on EFT, tests the effectiveness of the methods used in EFT. The only other couples therapy that is based significantly on research-tested methods is Integrative Behavioral Couples Therapy (IBCT). Recommended reading about IBCT is: Christensen, Andrew, and Neil S. Jacobson. *Reconcilable Differences.* New York: Guilford Press, 2000. As of the date of this publication, some significant research on Imago Relationship Therapy has begun but isn't comparable to the amount of research used in EFT, IBCT, or the Gottman method.

During their stay at the lab, couples wore a biofeedback harness similar to what astronauts wear in space to measure heart rate and oxygen in the bloodstream. The couple then engaged in all their normal activities together as live video and biometric data were recorded. The data from the biofeedback instruments was superimposed onto the video of the couple, so that physiological signs of distress—such as microfacial expressions—could be seen on the video as they were actually happening. Video segments of the couple's interactions were meticulously analyzed by researchers. From watching the video, researchers were able to log nearly every emotion that was expressed by both partners. They categorized emotions based on existing research about body language and tone of voice. Scores were given to each partner according to the data collected. Then Gottman and his associates conducted periodic relationship assessments with each couple for decades—up to thirty years in some cases—to find out if they stayed together. Based on the outcome of the relationship (happily married, married unhappily, divorced), conclusions were drawn about the physiological and behavioral data they had collected. Eventually, a pattern emerged. It became clear that certain behaviors and emotional states were significantly linked to couples either staying together or getting divorced. The Gottman Method Couples Therapy, which stems from these findings, methodically teaches you to identify when you're exhibiting signs of eminent marital catastrophe (Gottman calls these the *Four Horsemen of the Apocalypse),* and helps you form new patterns (the *Sound Relationship House*) that predict a secure future together.

If it weren't for the fact that Gottman married Julie Schwartz, a marriage therapist, it's possible that little of the data he collected would have been used to actually help couples. Before he met Julie, John had devoted his career to working mathematically—strictly with statistics, data, and research. He researched couples for decades but never took much interest in actually helping the subjects of his studies. Joking about this recently, he said, "I didn't want to help people, I wanted to study them. When I met Julie, she wanted to help people. So we compromised and started helping people."

Dr. Gottman is the author of 190 published academic articles and is author or coauthor of forty books. He's relevant to our discussion about the most effective couples therapies especially because of his collaboration with his wife, Julie— together they developed a method to teach couples the skills needed to stay happily married. Starting in the early 1990s, Gottman worked with others to develop rigorous scientific procedures (including the videotaping at the Love Lab) for predicting relationship success and failure. This information was a treasure trove to Julie. Her passion was providing couples with effective tools to repair their relationships and help them thrive. When Julie began collaborating professionally with her husband, they opened a creative floodgate. Together they created a system for treating relationship problems based on what they referred to in their research as the "Masters" and the "Disasters," the former being the most successful and satisfied couples, and the latter the couples that were the most dissatisfied or had ended their relationship.

In 1996, John and Julie Gottman founded The Gottman

Institute. By the 1999 publication of *The Marriage Clinic: A Scientifically Based Marital Therapy,* they had established themselves as among the world's leading authorities on training couples therapists in evidence-based interventions.

WHAT TO EXPECT WHEN VISITING A GOTTMAN METHOD COUPLES THERAPIST

There are three goals in Gottman Method Couples Therapy. The first is to identify and stop behaviors that research has identified as highly toxic to relationships. The second is to create what Gottman calls "shared meaning." The third is to build a closer friendship.

If you read books about Gottman Method Couples Therapy, it's easy to conclude this therapy is one of the more formulaic types of couples therapy among the three therapies described in this book. It has a matter-of-fact, data-driven feel to it because of the heavy influence of Gottman's scientific research with couples. However, sitting down with a Gottman therapist feels anything but formulaic; Gottman therapists are trained to gather information and provide guidance and advice in such a way that you don't feel dependent on having a therapist present to have productive conversations.

People with less affinity for "touchy feely" therapy approaches tend to like the way that the Gottman method uses practical labels for feelings. One husband commented that he liked not having to think of himself sharing his feelings with his wife. Instead, the husband used the Gottman term for feeling attached, *turning toward*, and said "all I'm doing is 'turning toward you,' and that seems much more manageable than sharing my feelings." Despite the pragmatic feel of Gottman Method Couples Therapy, it's still clearly an attachment-based therapy; its goal is to provide a safe environment where you and your partner can learn how to be vulnerable with each other while sustaining nurturing attitudes that will help you repair your relationship.

Gottman Method therapists are trained to pay attention to subtle details that indicate how you and your partner communicate. Your therapist will actively guide your conversation, monitoring and helping you with the way you discuss topics. In particular, he or she is listening for signs of the *Four Horsemen of the Apocalypse*: Criticism, Contempt, Defensiveness, and Stonewalling. Dr. Gottman found that if these events occur frequently in your relationship, unless you seek professional intervention, you're headed for marital disaster. His studies showed that the Four Horsemen predict early divorce—an average of 5.6 years after the wedding. Emotional withdrawal and anger can predict later divorce—an average of 16.2 years after the wedding. In contrast, research shows that couples who receive professional support to deal with the Four Horsemen maintain a stable relationship for many years after intervention.[35]

---

35   *Effects on marriage of a psycho-education intervention with couples undergoing the transition to parenthood, evaluation at 1-year post-intervention,* Shapiro, A.F., and Gottman, J.M., (2005); *Journal of Family Communication,* 5(1), 1-24; Halchuk, R., Makinen, J. & Johnson, S.M. (2010) Resolving Attachment Injuries in Couples using Emotionally Focused Therapy: A 3 Year Follow-up. *Journal of Couple and Relationship Therapy,* 9, 31-47.

JOHN GOTTMAN'S FOUR HORSEMEN OF THE APOCALYPSE

Gottman's research predicted divorce in couples that showed criticism, contempt, defensiveness, and stonewalling, aptly nicknamed the "Four Horsemen of the Apocalypse." The good news is that couples therapy successfully changed the apocalyptic outcome and saved most relationships.

Criticism: Stating complaints by identifying them as a defect in one's partner's personality; that is, giving the partner negative trait attributions. Example: "You always talk about yourself. You are so selfish."

Contempt: Statements that come from a relative position of superiority. Contempt is the greatest predictor of divorce and must be eliminated. Example: "You're an idiot."

Defensiveness: Self-protection in the form of righteous indignation or innocent victimhood. Defensiveness wards off a perceived attack. Example: "It's not my fault that we're always late; it's your fault."

Stonewalling: Emotional withdrawal from interaction. Example: The listener does not give the speaker the usual nonverbal signals that the listener is "tracking" the speaker.

You may find that experienced therapists who practice Gottman-style treatment are able to teach the many concepts of Gottman principles without lecturing or correcting you directly. By virtue of the kind of questions that the therapist asks and the choices he or she makes to support you and your partner during difficult moments, a Gottman therapist likes to be thought of as the rudder of the boat: you and your partner do the rowing while the therapist steers. As such, a Gottman therapist may act more like a coach during therapy. "I like for couples to go home and feel like they can have the kind of productive interaction they had during the session. I don't want them to feel like they need me to make it all happen," says Scott Wolfe, PhD, a Gottman therapist who trains therapists in the Gottman method.

Your therapist is likely to favor having you fill out extensive written questionnaires. They'd rather get as much information up front about the history of your relationship and the way you think about its problems instead of waiting for that information to be shared naturally—if ever—during the weeks or months you attend sessions.

You might hear your therapist cite research and explain the reasons behind strategies he or she suggests. But the real meat of the Gottman approach isn't just educating you about helpful facts. There's no quiz. Like the other two leading brands of couples therapies this book focuses on, the main focus of Gottman Couples Therapy is repairing and firing up the brain's natural attachment mechanism. You'll gradually learn how to *turn toward* your partner with respect and a nurturing attitude instead of avoiding or attacking each other.[36]

SUCCESSFUL COUPLES FIGHT, BUT FAIRLY

One of the most surprising discoveries made during Gottman's research is that there's no "right" way for couples to create and enjoy successful long-term relationships. Couples were followed for up to thirty years after they were first observed in the Love Lab. What the research found was that key elements must be present in successful relationships. But like voices in a chorus, there can be lots of variation in how the elements blend together to create harmony. This finding was contrary to what most relationship therapies taught. For example, it was once a "law" of couples therapy that anger was always harmful to relationships; all efforts were to be made to reduce expressions of anger to one's partner. However, Gottman's studies showed that couples could get really steamed at each other and still thrive as a couple in the long run—as long as the anger wasn't mixed in with resentment or contempt and repairs were frequently made. If you frequently felt deep down as though you were a better person than your partner—a sign of

---

36   Gottman's research doesn't directly reference attachment in much detail but instead uses more technical language to describe attachment concepts. For example, Gottman observed a phenomenon he called "Positive Sentiment Override (PSO.)" In a nutshell, PSO is feeling more warm, mushy feelings about your partner than prickly or harsh feelings. There's a lot more to PSO than this simple definition, but the importance of PSO is clear: according to Gottman, the goal of couples therapy should be to remove behaviors and habits that erode attachment, and to boost those that stimulate attachment.

contempt—then without intervention you were highly likely either to be divorced or highly dissatisfied with your relationship in four years' time.

Gottman's research asserts that successful couples don't always take turns listening "nicely" to each other—nor do they always use "I" statements. Building communication skills is a major part of Gottman couples therapy, but Gottman showed that it takes more than just following the steps of a communication exercise to still be married twenty years later. His research showed that couples may interrupt each other and get quite upset, but if they maintain an internal attitude of respect and openness, they'll be able to start and end arguments softly. This is key to having long-term success as a couple.

STAYING OUT OF THE "ROACH MOTEL" FOR COUPLES

Why is it that couples can get angry and fight and still remain together, happy and satisfied, many years later? Some couples keep bouncing back from hard times together. Other couples get angry and fight, but separate or divorce within four years. Gottman studied which concrete and observable factors made a difference in "successful" fights. He looked at couples for signs of what he called the *roach motel* effect. Like the slogan for the Black Flag insect poison, "Roaches check in, but they don't check out," certain couples become ensnared in a fatal tailspin of negativity. "They never get out of it alive," says Gottman, meaning the relationship doesn't last.

How do you stay out of the roach motel with your

committed partner? Research shows that to make a relationship last, you and your partner must find meaningful ways to stay attached. A couple's bond may be broken by hurt, disappointment, or resentment. But Gottman showed that, even in the case of abusive relationships—after the help of professional intervention—it's possible to tap into the drive to attach, to become better friends, learn to manage conflict, and to create ways to support each other's hopes for the future. The Gottman Method will first teach you to identify if you're in the roach motel, and then how to get out of it. First, you need to eliminate the Four Horsemen (Criticism, Contempt, Defensiveness, and Stonewalling) from your relationship. Second, you build a relationship that's resilient and based on behaviors used by successful couples that stay together. To guide you, the Gottman Method calls these principles the *Sound Relationship House*, or the Seven Ingredients of Successful Couples (see inset).

Your therapist will be skilled at helping you get out of the roach motel of negativity and create the positive habits that Gottman's research shows predict a long and satisfying relationship. After all, you don't want to hear the hoof beats of the Four Horsemen of the Apocalypse galloping through your love life. The simple concepts of the Sound Relationship House can give you and your partner a clear set of goals for how to construct or repair a love to last a long time. And for those of you who may be worried about being too vulnerable and open during the therapy process, you'll be comforted that the Gottman Method's concrete approach is grounded firmly in research and consists of easily teachable concepts.

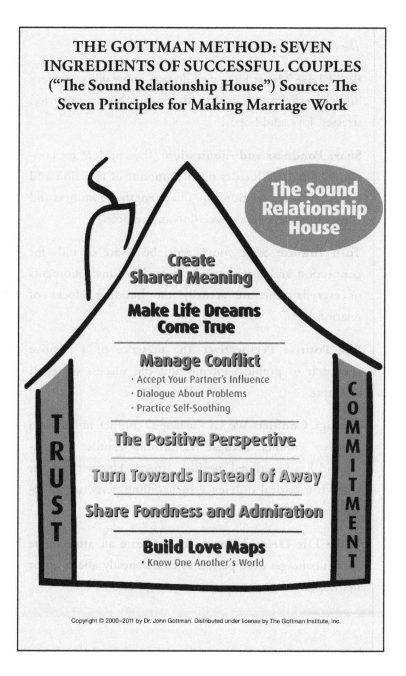

THE GOTTMAN METHOD: SEVEN
INGREDIENTS OF SUCCESSFUL COUPLES
("The Sound Relationship House") Source: The
Seven Principles for Making Marriage Work

The Sound
Relationship
House

Create
Shared Meaning

Make Life Dreams
Come True

Manage Conflict
· Accept Your Partner's Influence
· Dialogue About Problems
· Practice Self-Soothing

The Positive Perspective

Turn Towards Instead of Away

Share Fondness and Admiration

Build Love Maps
· Know One Another's World

T R U S T

C O M M I T M E N T

The Sound Relationship House (continued)

Build Love Maps: How well do you know your partner's inner psychological world, his or her history, worries, stresses, joys, and hopes?

Share Fondness and Admiration: The antidote for contempt, this level focuses on the amount of affection and respect within a relationship. (To strengthen fondness and admiration, express appreciation and respect.)

Turn Toward: State your needs, be aware of bids for connection and turn towards them. The small moments of everyday life are actually the building blocks of relationship.

The Positive Perspective: The presence of a positive approach to problem-solving and the success of repair attempts.

Manage Conflict: We say "manage" conflict rather than "resolve" conflict, because relationship conflict is natural and has functional, positive aspects. Understand that there is a critical difference in handling perpetual problems and solvable problems.

Make Life Dreams Come True: Create an atmosphere that encourages each person to talk honestly about his or her hopes, values, convictions and aspirations.

Create Shared Meaning: Understand important visions, narratives, myths, and metaphors about your relationship.

Trust: This is the state that occurs when a person knows that his or her partner acts and thinks to maximize that person's interests, and maximize that person's benefits, not just the partner's own interests and benefits. In other words, this means, "my partner has my back and is there for me."

Commitment: This means believing (and acting on the belief) that your relationship with this person is completely your lifelong journey, for better or for worse (meaning that if it gets worse you will both work to improve it). It implies cherishing your partner's positive qualities and nurturing gratitude by comparing the partner favorably with real or imagined others, rather than trashing the partner by magnifying negative qualities, and nurturing resentment by comparing unfavorably with real or imagined others.

KIERA AND JED TURN TO A GOTTMAN THERAPIST FOR HELP

Kiera and Jed met in graduate school, when Kiera was going through a bad breakup. Jed was a confidant of Kiera's other friend, and one especially awful day after her breakup, Kiera reached out to Jed for emotional support. His warmth and kindness during that time made a big impression on her.

Soon thereafter, Jed and Kiera grew closer and actually

spent more time together than Kiera spent with her girlfriend. The friend finally helped Kiera realize that she had become close with a really stable, quality guy. "So why are you just friends with him?" her girlfriend asked. Kiera thought about that. Why *was* she just friends with him? One day, feeling playful, Kiera startled Jed by kissing him. That was six years ago. They'd been together ever since.

Jed and Kiera's dating progressed slowly. They saw each other frequently for a year before becoming exclusive, then dated another four years before getting engaged. Kiera asked Jed many times when he was going to pop the question. Just as Kiera hadn't thought about taking their relationship further before her girlfriend asked her why she and Jed were just friends, it almost didn't occur to Jed that they could progress to a deeper level of intimacy while dating. Jed could drag his feet when making big decisions, and that made Kiera uneasy. But once they finally agreed to get married, Jed grew excited. He got involved in the wedding details. After a twelve-month engagement, they were married near their alma mater in Virginia.

Over the next few years, Jed and Kiera had two kids. They were both busy working and raising their family until Kiera lost her job. As she put it, "I almost lost my mind too." She began having panic attacks that started when she would try to look for new job openings each morning. There were few jobs available for her. She and Jed could not afford childcare on one salary, and the kids needed her constant attention. Kiera felt like a failure as a professional and struggled to be attentive to her children. By the time Jed came home from work, she'd vent to him about everything that was going wrong. Jed remembered it this way: "It wasn't just that she was sharing with me how her day went or maybe that she was having a rough time. She saw *everything*—even little things—as elaborate catastrophes waiting to happen."

Kiera began individual psychotherapy. Her therapist helped her develop mindfulness techniques to feel more connected to and in control of her body, and these exercises triggered a soothing, relaxed feeling. She devoted herself to doing the exercises and said they were like daily doses of medicine for her. She enjoyed the stillness and the lasting effect that a few weeks of mindfulness relaxation exercises—her "un-jam sessions," as she called them—had on her. The panic attacks became fewer and farther apart, then stopped altogether. She began to feel alive again. Never one to sit still, Kiera surprised Jed with her enthusiastic embrace of the "less is more" philosophy of mindfulness practices.

However, it wasn't long after Kiera's self-described "salvation" through her own therapy that she and Jed began having real problems. He began feeling jealous of her and became easily frustrated by her new routines and mantras. From his perspective, they seemed to come out of nowhere. Kiera wanted Jed to talk to a therapist of his own to help him deal better with his frustration, but he was adamantly against it. He couldn't see the point in paying to talk to a stranger. He much preferred shooting pool with his guy friends or having a few beers to make himself feel better. Sometimes one of his friends brought marijuana and shared it with Jed. Jed and Kiera's diverging areas of interest became a major bone of contention, and this led to frequent blowout fights.

Kiera resented Jed's sharp refusal to experiment with therapy—something that meant so much to her—but underneath the resentment was her feeling of being ignored and alone. She began to think that Jed was never going to understand her. Old memories resurfaced. She wondered why, for example, he seemed so indifferent about getting serious when they were first dating. It left her with a haunting feeling that they weren't really meant to be together.

Discussing the situation with her therapist one day, Kiera explained Jed's resistance to therapy. "He won't do it," she told him, "because he thinks what I learned in my therapy is to blame for our disagreements. It's like he's got something against me getting better." Her therapist told her about the methodical approach and scientific basis of the Gottman Method. He recommended it to Kiera because he thought the matter-of-fact, research-driven style would appeal to each of them, especially Jed. At first, Jed dismissed the idea of going to therapy with Kiera. But after considering the thought of her going without him—which she told him she would do—he reluctantly agreed.

The next day Kiera called Christine, a couples therapist certified in the Gottman Method. After a short interview over the phone, she booked an appointment and was told to download several questionnaires before coming to the first session.

JED AND KIERA GET TO THE HEART OF THEIR CONFLICT AND FIND HOPE

In the initial session, Christine told Kiera and Jed that she was very glad they'd come to see her. She said the answers each of them gave on the questionnaires showed signs that concerned her about the amount of negativity in their relationship, but she was confident she could help them find a way to improve it.

The first three sessions with Christine were used to conduct a thorough assessment. The first week, they met with Christine as a couple for eighty minutes. The next week, they met individually in fifty-minute, one-on-one private sessions. Jed was impressed by the extensive attention that Christine gave to gathering information. It helped him build confidence that she could formulate the correct course of therapy for them. It also gave him the sense that the therapy was about more than just talking about feelings "just for the sake of talking." They dutifully answered a lot of questions, both in the oral interviews and in several questionnaires Christine had them fill out.

Christine explained to Jed and Kiera that electronically measuring their stress levels during therapy was an important part of her work with couples. Jed was intrigued by the idea of biofeedback and thought it was a novel idea to rig each of them up to a pulse oximeter—a small device that slides over one finger and measures heart rate and blood oxygen levels. Christine conducted baseline tests to establish a relaxed, resting measurement, then set the oximeter's alarm to ring if blood oxygen content went below 95 percent or if the heart rate exceeded one hundred beats per minute. Christine told them that the alarm meant their body was tense and producing stress-inducing chemicals like adrenaline, which is known to severely inhibit new learning and listening. "This alarm going off," Christine reassured them, "doesn't mean you're doing something wrong. It just means you're not doing anything therapeutic at that moment. You're paying me for therapy, so I use this tool to tell me when I need to help you relax at critical moments together. Normally, you'd just escalate, which is not productive at all."

Christine asked Jed and Kiera questions that invited them to tell their story about the relationship, from the very beginning. Kiera had her version, Jed had his. Christine listened carefully and took lots of notes. She wanted to know how they met, what the first year of their marriage was like, and what they remembered about major transitions such as the birth of their children.

During their fourth meeting, as a couple, Christine told Kiera and Jed that she wanted to focus on a major problem that seemed to be apparent in their relationship. She discussed how important it is to start a controversial conversation with politeness and without harsh criticism or contempt. She showed video clips on her computer of couples starting off conversations on the wrong foot. One woman addressed her husband by saying "What's wrong with you? Can't you figure out how to fix the television?" Christine then showed clips of people using a "soft start-up" to a conversation. These people were able to keep the focus on themselves and to voice their needs clearly and with basic politeness—complaining but not blaming. In one couple, the husband pointed out that he was unhappy with his wife's choice of words when talking to one of their children. "I don't want to step on your toes here, but I wish there was a way you could encourage Josephine when you're correcting her. I want her to know right and wrong but I don't want her to feel put down when we correct her."

Gottman's research showed that couples were highly likely to stay together a long time if they could do soft start-ups about difficult topics. She said that it's important for both partners to approach each other with a soft start-up, but it was slightly more predictive of success if women, in particular, used a soft start-up with men. Similarly, Christine pointed out that men who were able to accept influence from their wives reaped large margins in terms of maintaining a successful relationship. "Accepting influence" simply means that you ask your partner's opinion about decisions that are important to him or her. You listen and allow her input to change your decision in significant ways. At this point, Jed interrupted Christine.

"I don't know what you mean, Christine. I think I listen to Kiera all the time. I can't *help* but listen to her."

"Jed," said Christine, "right then when you said that, it seemed to me that you were kind of feeling something—what is it, exasperation maybe?" Christine's training in the Gottman method told her how important it is to identify feelings like contempt or resentment lurking in the quick back-and-forth conversations between partners.

"Yeah, exactly," said Jed.

"It sounds like you're saying that you listen to Kiera, but inside, you have a negative feeling about it?" asked Christine.

"Yes. It feels like sometimes I don't have a choice."

"Well," said Christine, "This is so important. I want to help you with this. You're trying to listen, but you've got mixed feelings as you're doing it. You're feeling resentful but going through the motions of listening."

"You're totally right," said Jed. "Sometimes I even mock her, to myself. If I say what I'm thinking, it's not always nice." Christine reassured Jed that his feelings were valid—that this happens all the time to couples in "gridlock" about an issue— and also told Kiera that she knew this wasn't easy on her either. Christine mentioned research identifying that 69 percent of the things that couples argue about are ultimately unsolvable problems—meaning it's better to focus on the 31 percent that are solvable and learn to live with the rest. She also cautioned about negative feelings like resentment, and how it's critically important to find the source of resentment and release it—to make peace and let go of things you can't change.

Christine helped Jed slow his breathing—his pulse oximeter showed that his body had reached a state of hyperarousal in reaction to feeling threatened. She also spent time carefully interviewing Jed about how his concerns had turned into resentment. She highlighted what she called his "hidden wish" behind his disappointment. Jed's countenance shifted noticeably as he shared—with Christine's guidance—his wish that Kiera would acknowledge his ability to provide for the family and to make Kiera feel better. Christine would refer often in therapy to the Gottman Method's Dream Within Conflict exercise, which could help them look beyond their immediate surface conflict for hidden wishes.

Jed's unexpressed wish was that Kiera would rely on him more instead of turning to her self-help programs. As a teenager, Jed's sister had become terminally ill with leukemia.

Before her illness, she and Jed weren't particularly close, but after she became ill Jed never left her side. He became used to sacrificing his needs for his sister's until she literally died in his arms. As Kiera listened to Jed open up to her about the pain of losing his sister, something clicked for her. For the first time, she could understand how seeking self-help activities could feel, to Jed, like a rejection of his caretaking instinct.

Jed appreciated that Christine didn't over-emphasize the Dreams Within Conflict exercise. He could tolerate little doses of sharing vulnerable feelings—and doing so made him feel closer to Kiera—but too much "soft stuff" made him feel foolish. Christine pointed out that witnessing each other's dreams was a good first step, but that for many couples, more concrete habits needed to be established to lower the overall temperature of conflict. "Like the Spanish proverb," said Christine, "Love is a furnace but it won't cook the stew." She wanted to show Kiera and Jed a habit that could help each be gentler with the other, creating conditions that would favor sharing wishes and hopes without strings attached. She turned to Jed.

"I want to show you how you can be a good listener without expending a ton of energy. A lot of people think listening means reacting to what someone's saying. You don't need to fix whatever feelings Kiera is sharing with you. But listening without reacting—just saying 'I get it,' is often what partners, especially women, want the most. But you can't be totally passive either. For example, I want you to remember that she needs some sort of basic acknowledgement that you're breathing and alive while she's talking to you. You don't have to agree with or like what she's saying. Just let her know you're alive and there with her."

"Really?" asked Jed skeptically. "I don't have to agree?"

"Nope. You don't have to agree at all. Just say, 'I hear you' or 'Hold on, let me get to a place where I can hear what you're saying.' Just let her know she's not crazy and that she's important to you. Don't get hung up on what she's saying to you. That may be counterintuitive, I know, but just focus on the fact that she is saying something to you. Don't try to solve her problems. Just be with her and let her know you're with her, that you have a pulse."

"Ok, let me get this straight," said Jed. "I think you're kind of saying that I need to give her total acknowledgement, let her talk. And just letting her talk will make her feel better?"

"Exactly," said Christine. "But in fact, it's not just talking that makes her feel better. It's when you accept her influence."

"Well, I'm confused," said Jed. "I thought I didn't have to agree with her?"

"You don't," replied Christine. "Accepting influence can mean a lot of things. If you can't agree, then it means that you care enough about her that you'll at least acknowledge her when she's trying to talk. You won't stonewall her or dismiss her because you disagree."

Jed made an effort to put Christine's advice into practice. Christine coached him during the sessions, which helped him understand that it wasn't very hard to implement the idea of accepting influence from Kiera. His behavior was reinforced because he could see it had a very big effect on her. Kiera told him how nice it was to really feel his interest in her. She even admitted that a lot of things she insisted were "musts" were really distorted exaggerations based on feeling that she couldn't get through to him. With Christine's help, Jed and Kiera were feeling much more hopeful about working things out together. They made fast progress and had confronted two of The Four Horsemen of the Apocalypse—criticism and stonewalling—and by the fourth conjoint session, Christine felt they were ready to focus on building more positive connections with each other.

HOW JED AND KIERA BUILT A STRONGER BOND

Now that Jed and Kiera had a working understanding of how to stop some of the behaviors that were most threatening to their survival as a couple, Christine wanted to help them develop a more secure connection to each other. She gave them some worksheets that described the concept of the Sound Relationship House and told them that she'd like them to do some exercises at home before the next session.

Christine gave them a "Love Maps" questionnaire, which prompted each of them to rate how familiar they believed their partner was with certain areas of his or her life. Some of the true/false questions were:

- I can name my partner's best friends.

- I can tell you about my partner's basic philosophy of life.

- I can list my partner's favorite three movies.

- I know my partner's major current worries.

- I can tell you, in detail, my first impressions of my partner.

When Jed and Kiera came back into the next session, Christine first checked to see if there had been any difficult fights or "regrettable incidents" in the interim. They'd had a major disagreement about how to enforce limits with their four-year-old, so with Christine's help, they discussed it again, minus the criticism and stonewalling that had blocked them during the week. Kiera was able to talk about her irritation with Jed by using a soft start-up. In that way, she stood up for herself without putting Jed down. "You have a good point," Jed told Kiera, even though he didn't totally agree. He was able to accept her influence—she wanted him to reinforce the limits she set with their daughter—and Jed was able to look her in the eye and give a simple validation instead of rolling his eyes and walking away the way he might normally do.

In the remaining thirty minutes of the session, Christine introduced a card game for them to play together that would increase their awareness of each other's inner life. Research revealed, she explained, that the *masters of relationships* had a large cognitive "map" of their partner's world. The goal of the game was to increase the size of their mental love maps by asking each other open-ended questions that couldn't be answered with a "yes" or "no." By doing so, Christine told them, their lives would feel more interconnected even if they had different interests.

One at a time, Jed and Kiera asked each other some of the questions they'd been polled about in their homework questionnaires. Kiera pulled a card that read, "What is your partner's favorite way to spend an evening?" Jed pulled a card that read,

"What turns your partner on sexually?" They each laughed at the coincidence of these two questions and playfully did their best to give an answer. "The goal," said Christine, "is not to get a 'right' answer, but to start a conversation where you share more details." Some of the questions they answered quickly; others took more time and stirred up stronger feelings. Jed confessed that at first, the idea of doing something so proscribed felt like a drag to him, but he was now glad their sessions had clear agendas. He felt like there was purpose to their visits. "Maybe," he said to Kiera before the end of the session, "this means we won't just be ships passing in the night anymore?" Kiera's face lit up with a huge smile. They were heading in the right direction and had clearly found a therapist who used a type of couples therapy that was compatible with their own needs.

IS THE GOTTMAN METHOD OUR STYLE?

Do you want to know if the Gottman Method Couples Therapy is for you? Take a look at the features below that differentiate this method of couples therapy from others. Keep in mind that some therapists use the Gottman Method techniques all the time, but others may only use them when they are the best choice for your situation. It's critical that you ask your therapist how closely he or she adheres to the "pure" Gottman Method approach, if that's important to you.

Gottman Method Couples Therapy is unique because:

- It's a couples therapy based on the observational

research of the University of Seattle's Gottman Love Lab. Gottman and collaborators used hours of video and biometric monitoring of couples' interactions and kept track of the outcome of their relationships for more than two decades. The Gottmans created their couples therapy techniques based on the behaviors they saw in successful couples (i.e. ones that stayed together and reported satisfaction).[37]

- It makes extensive use of collecting data from you and your partner before, during, and sometimes after therapy. You can usually expect questionnaires and may possibly be expected to use a pulse oximeter to measure stress in your body during sessions.

- It's an attachment-based couples therapy because it uses methods designed to bring you closer together as partners and friends and to manage conflict. You're likely to be asked about some past relationships,

---

37 The Gottman Method Couples Therapy is considered a "scientifically based" therapy, but the actual outcomes from Gottman therapy have not been significantly studied. Since 1972, Gottman researchers have studied more than 3,000 couples—perhaps more than any other single group of researchers to date—at the University of Indiana, the University of Illinois, and the University of Washington. Although Gottman researchers have observed and chronicled the behavior of couples, they haven't included outcome studies that test the effectiveness of Gottman couples therapy. In contrast, Emotionally Focused Therapy has conducted and published extensive research that specifically validates the outcomes of using EFT. (Integrative Behavioral Couples Therapy (IBCT) is one other method—not described in this book—that also has a significant body of outcome-validated methods of couples therapy.) Imago Relationship Therapy continues to build on a small but promising amount of outcome research of Imago methods.

including childhood relationships, but the focus tends to be on building new, positive habits together and learning to live with unchangeable differences.

FITTING-ROOM QUIZ

Answer these questions to see if the Gottman Method might be a good fit for you and your partner:

A. Are you open to being "tested" by your therapist, answering 1–2 hours of questionnaires at the beginning of therapy, and possibly using live biometric feedback during sessions?

1. Yes, I'd rather that my therapist gets all the information about us quickly and efficiently.

2. I don't have a big preference for how my therapist gathers information…but I like structured questionnaires.

3. I'd prefer sharing information orally, as it's needed, but I'm on board with filling out questionnaires if it's helpful.

4. I don't want to fill out questionnaires. I'd rather just talk about our issues.

B. Is it important that the couples therapy you're doing be based on research linked to claims of being able to predict divorce?

1. Absolutely, there's no room for guessing about what works and what doesn't.

2. This sounds important; I'm definitely intrigued.

3. Research-based information is nice but not the most important part of couples therapy to me.

4. It's more important to find a therapist who clicks with us than one who knows all the "right" answers.

C. How would you feel if, after you've raised an important issue about your relationship, your therapist responds by pulling out a worksheet and asking you to learn the relevant concepts of a new exercise?

1. This is perfect—I love concrete learning and will do anything that helps me get more clarity.

2. Having an expert personally guide us through exercises is invaluable and productive, but it's also nice to just talk "person-to-person."

3. I'd really rather not be "exercised" all the time, but this would be valuable for the right situation.

4. I could buy a book that gives me exercises, but I'm paying a therapist to deliver a more conversational interaction.

D. How comfortable are you with this statement: "Sixty-nine percent of all problems between your partner and you are basically irresolvable. The important part is how you live with what you can't change and focus on what you can change."

1. Hand me some lemons and I'll make lemonade.

2. I aspire to live this, but need lots of help remembering.

3. This makes sense, but there are other ways to look at it too.

4. I don't give up easily. Accepting the unacceptable is unacceptable to me.

E. Are you interested in learning how to become better friends with your partner and in being able to turn to him or her when you're distressed?

1. Sign me up! This is why we're going to couples therapy.

2. Being better friends is high on my list.

3. I could see how this would be helpful but I'm interested in other solutions too.

4. I don't see how being better friends will solve our problems.

How to Score Your Answers

Add the numbers you chose for your answers, and then use the chart below to determine what kind of match Gottman

Method Couples Therapy is for you. Do the same for your partner's score, and use the fit rating to further assess your compatibility with this brand of therapy.

Just Right: If your total is 5–10, it's a great fit, and you'll likely be intrigued by the Gottman Method. Strongly consider finding a therapist who uses this kind of therapy.

Loose Fit: If your total is 11–15, it's a decent fit, but some aspects of the Gottman Method may not thrill you. You might want to look into Gottman therapy and possibly compare with an alternative to be sure.

Tight Squeeze: If your total is 16–20, you could be more annoyed by than receptive to the Gottman Method. Proceed with caution, and interview potential therapists carefully. Feel free to work with a Gottman therapist if he or she uses the approach judiciously and perhaps in combination with other methods that are a better fit for you—perhaps from either Emotionally Focused Therapy or the Imago Relationship Therapy.

Keep in mind that this "fit-ness" test is a very rough guide. Just like clothing sizes that vary between manufacturers, you could find wide variation between any two Gottman therapists. Depending on the therapist's exposure to other significant couples therapy training, he or she may depend exclusively on using Gottman methods, or may use it only when it's a good fit.

FURTHER READING

J.M. Gottman, *The Science of Trust: Emotional Attunement for Couples* (New York: W.W. Norton, 2011).

J. M. Gottman and J. DeClaire, *The Relationship Cure.* (New York: Crown Publishing, 2001).

J.M. Gottman and N. Silver, *The Seven Principles for Making Marriage Work* (New York: Crown Publishing, 1999).

J.M. Gottman and N. Silver, *Why Marriages Succeed or Fail: What You Can Learn from the Breakthrough Research to Make Your Marriage Last* (New York: Simon & Schuster, 2012).

J.M. Gottman, J.S. Gottman, and J. Declaire, *Ten Lessons to Transform Your Marriage* (New York: Three Rivers Press, 2006).

CHAPTER 6

EMOTIONALLY FOCUSED THERAPY FOR COUPLES

"When people feel loved, they are freer, more alive, and more powerful than we ever imagined."

—Dr. Susan Johnson,
co-creator of Emotionally Focused Therapy for Couples

AS THE FOUNDER of one of the fastest-growing methods of couples therapy today, Emotionally Focused Therapy for couples (EFT), Dr. Susan Johnson recalls the era in psychology's not-so-distant past when "emotion" was considered a dirty word. Johnson is one of the most influential researchers in the field of couples therapy, and she has been at the vanguard of the "attachment revolution." Her work has offered a viable alternative to rational/behavioral methods of therapy widely considered pre-eminent during the recent decades of managed care.

Like the other therapies detailed in this book, you'll find variation among therapists who practice EFT for couples. Here are some of the main features of EFT and what you can usually expect during your work with most therapists trained in this approach:

- EFT is a couples therapy method validated by more than twenty years of empirical research.[38] Ninety percent of couples receiving EFT rated themselves higher in satisfaction than couples receiving no treatment, and 70–73 percent of couples surveyed after therapy were "recovered from distress" at follow-up.[39]

---

38   There is one other kind of therapy not detailed in this book that has significant empirical research, Behavioral Couples Therapy (BCT). Integrative Behavioral Couples Therapy (IBCT) also has significant empirical research. In the past ten years, the popularity of EFT has skyrocketed. It has developed a reputation as one of the leading couples therapies. Both the Gottman Method Couples Therapy and EFT are based on research, but there's a difference: Gottman Method is a "research-informed couples therapy," while Emotion-Focused Therapy (EFT) is an outcome research–based couples therapy. "Research-informed" means that the methods that the Gottmans designed for use in couples therapy were based on scientific (observed and measured) studies about the behavior of couples in general. Outcome research, done extensively on EFT, tests the effectiveness of the methods used in EFT.

By comparison, Imago Relationship Therapy still requires more substantial research before it can be considered a research-based therapy like EFT. Existing research based on Imago is highly promising and shows positive outcomes from the therapy, but the research is limited by a lack of a control groups (couples in distress that are willing to forgo therapy so they can be compared to couples that are actively getting therapy). Very few psychotherapy studies with control groups exist because of how difficult it is to find willing participants. Therefore, EFT is unique in that it has conducted empirical research with control groups.

39   According to the International Centre for Excellence in Emotionally Focused Therapy (ICEEFT).

- As an attachment-based couples therapy, EFT focuses on building opportunities for bonding between you and your partner.

- Your therapist will focus attention on how you experience your emotions. Rather than simply naming or reframing negative emotions, you'll be shown how to experience emotions in a way that can produce important changes in your relationship.

HEART AND SOUL: USING THE POWER OF PRIMARY EMOTIONS

Emotionally Focused Therapy is so named because of the attention placed on universal "primary emotions"—our vulnerability, innocence, and creativity—that are often buried in struggles between spouses or partners. By harnessing the energy of primary emotions, sometimes thought of as your "heart" or "soul," EFT gives you a way to interrupt the cycle of struggle that keeps you from enjoying a happy and successful relationship. The goal of EFT is to make couples more aware of subconscious patterns of interaction that evoke "secondary emotions"—protective reactions that limit vulnerability and diminish trust. Couples are given tools to interrupt these destructive, intimacy-limiting reactions, and are taught to evoke deeper primary emotions that promote bonding and connection.

STEPHANIE AND KARIM: SALVAGING A MARRIAGE AFTER INFIDELITY

Stephanie called an EFT therapist for help after she discovered that her husband, Karim, was having an affair. She discovered the affair when she was looking up a birthday invitation on Karim's computer. A link came up to a website that helped people find a partner interested in having an affair. Stephanie searched their phone records and found a number of late-night calls. She was so shocked she couldn't eat for three days. Karim admitted to going on "dates" with a few women and confessed that he had become sexually involved with one of them. When Stephanie started to make plans to go stay at her parents' house, Karim begged her to try couples counseling with him. He made some calls and his pastor recommended an EFT therapist named Stuart.

The minute Stephanie and Karim walked into Stuart's office, he knew they really needed his help. Stephanie hadn't stopped crying all week, and Karim looked like he'd just been plucked from a shipwreck at sea. Neither had slept much. It was their first time in couples therapy, and understandably they weren't sure what to ask or how to begin. Their lack of sleep put them in a complete fog.

After gathering some of the basics about their situation, Stuart decided it was important for him to start off by introducing Stephanie and Karim to how he thought he could help. He described his familiarity with the kind of situation they were facing and explained how he knew from experience that he could offer them remedies to give them a very good shot at getting back on their feet. "It's not going to be easy," he said, "but I know the way through this and am so glad that you made the call to find me."

"PLAYING BY FEEL" WITH EFT

Stuart's reassurance was especially helpful for Stephanie and Karim to hear. They were eager for specifics about how therapy was going to work and asked for advice about what to do next. Stuart described how EFT focuses on emotions. He said the method is especially distinct because of how it's designed to stimulate the brain's attachment instinct by using primary emotions, a term he went on to explain. He said that unlike some other couples therapies, he was not likely to give them cognitive exercises—common in solution-focused or cognitive-behavioral therapies—but instead preferred to coach them through their emotional states, moment-by-moment.

"It all comes down to feelings," he said. "I'm going to slow down some of the reactions you guys have when you're together that put you into a bad place."

Stephanie interrupted Stuart. "I don't understand what that means. All I know is he's contacting these women, and I had no idea. I'm hurt, I'm angry, and I'm confused. Are you going to be able to help us?"

Stuart let Stephanie know he understood how hard it must be to be in her shoes. He asked her to say more about what she was going through, and as she talked she became more and more agitated and angry. He calmly looked into her eyes, which were red from crying all week. They looked swollen and puffy and, despite her clear anger, it was also easy to see she was in pain. To her surprise, Stuart said he noticed the heaviness in her eyes and said he could see she was physically hurting as well. Stuart said that emotions have two sides. He was interested in her anger, but he especially wanted to talk more about her pain. He asked her what it was like for her to feel like that.

"Oh, God!" Stephanie moaned. "I must look like a drowned cat!"

"Really, it's okay," coached Stuart. "You're having a normal reaction to a very unusual amount of stress here. We're supposed to look this way if we're upset." He was letting Stephanie know he was comfortable with her showing her feelings, and that he wasn't concerned about appearances. He asked her to try to be comfortable with the way she felt and looked, at least during therapy. He said that emotions, even the ones that make us look like drowned cats, are part of being human and being real. Hearing this from anyone else would normally have made Stephanie cringe—*how could there be anything good about feeling and looking so wretched?* But from her therapist, Stuart's words came as a comfort and a relief. She had been to other therapists who might have tried to be helpful and said, "Oh, you look fine. Do you have any concealer in that bag?" With Stuart, she immediately sensed an authenticity that she welcomed. More than anything, she wanted to be able to let her guard down but was afraid and uncertain about how to do it. If she could be herself with Stuart, maybe she could learn how to be herself with Karim, she thought.

Stuart turned his attention to Karim. "What normally happens next when you see Stephanie so torn up like this?

How do you react?" Stuart had already begun using the most prevalent tool in EFT therapy, which is called *tracking the cycle*. It's a way to discuss what typically happens between you and your partner, without letting the back-and-forth reactions spin out of control. Stuart described and labeled each twist and turn of the couple's reactions to each other with a calmness that seemed to soak up the uneasiness between the two.

"Here's the thing," said Karim, his face beginning to flush, "I don't know how to react. What am I supposed to say? I know this hurts her a lot. But I'm over here feeling...I'm a mess myself. I don't have answers for her that she's going to like."

"So you're saying that you're feeling like a mess. You don't have answers, but you're saying 'Hey, what about me, I'm suffering too?'" Karim was nodding his head in agreement.

"So tell me about what you're going through," said Stuart to Karim. "Tell me more about the mess."

"It's definitely true that I'm trapped," said Karim. "It's really hard for me to listen to her when she's so upset. When I try to understand her, I don't get it right. When I get frustrated, mostly with myself, she jumps on me. So then I just want to run for the hills...it's easier to tune the whole thing out."

Stephanie chimed in to say that she knew that none of her feelings ever got through to Karim. When this had happened before, she'd become despondent and made jealous accusations about him cheating on her—before he was ever unfaithful. Karim, in response, escaped into his work and used his responsibility as a business owner to cover for his not wanting to spend time around Stephanie.

"When you tune her out," Stuart asked Karim, "What happens then?"

Stuart alternated between them, asking each in turn to describe their usual reactions to the other. Despite talking about extremely painful issues, the EFT process of tracking the cycle kept Stephanie and Karim in touch enough with their reactions to talk about them, but not so much that they were swept away by them. Before coming to see Stuart, they tried to have discussions about their feelings. It was a disaster. Both noticed how much easier it was to cover such volatile, emotional terrain with Stuart leading the way using EFT.

THE KEY TOOL OF EMOTIONALLY FOCUSED THERAPY: GETTING OFF THE MERRY-GO-ROUND

EFT's main philosophy is that relationships fail because they fall into a cyclical pattern of negative reactions. These erode intimacy and suck the life out of a partnership between two people. Relationship problems are the cumulative effect of unchecked negativity. EFT attempts to get you off the reactive merry-go-round, disrupt the chain reactions, and replace negativity with caring behaviors. An EFT therapist will be assertive about keeping the conversation focused objectively on where you are in your negative cycle—like a meteorologist talking about a weather system—without allowing you to blame each other or blame the relationship. In this, the approach is also similar to Imago and the Gottman Method. EFT makes frequent use of the term "negative cycle" and asks partners to share responsibility for changing it. Stuart knew that a couple dealing with infidelity has a lot of negative reactivity. With Stephanie and Karim, he was very persistent in his directives to keep them focused on details that would lead them out of the habits and reactions that kept them emotionally distant from each other.

You can expect an EFT therapist to make a conscious effort to build alliance and trust with you during the earliest sessions of therapy. Your therapist will likely favor open-ended, subjective questions that allow you to expand on your thoughts and feelings, in contrast to more structured styles of therapy that might give you a bit less room to simply talk freely. For example, objective questionnaires (true/false questions) are typically used to guide conversations in the early sessions of Gottman Method couples therapy. And during many Imago sessions, the therapist uses intentional dialogue—a highly structured communication exercise—to purposefully focus your conversation in specific ways. Normally, Stuart used the first three sessions with a couple to gather relevant historical information and context about the relationship and any concerns. But because Stephanie and Karim were in the midst of dealing with a crisis, he wanted to immediately talk about their "cycle," the pattern of emotional reactions that was typical of their relationship.

As Stuart gathered impressions from Stephanie and Karim, he also began to define their problems by referring to events as "the negative loop." Objectively labeling the pattern of negativity is designed to de-escalate blame and to create an atmosphere that feels collaborative. "Together," he told them at the end of their first session, "the three of us will begin to dismantle the negative loop and replace it with new habits that work better for both of you."

Couples can feel very hopeful when hearing their problems reframed as a "negative loop" or "cycle" that can be dismantled together. Unlike one of Hollywood's favorite versions of couples therapy, in which the therapist pounces on deviant spouse behavior like a litigator in court, you won't be attacked by the therapist or your partner during EFT therapy. EFT therapists are trained to see the problems you're having as the symptoms of painful but nevertheless normal and highly treatable causes. And because EFT therapists are so attuned to emotion, the therapy tends to work well even for people who think they're incapable of talking about their feelings, such as men and women who are unenthusiastic about therapy. In fact, there's research on EFT that suggests it works especially well for men whose spouses consider them "inexpressive."[40]

When they started EFT, Stephanie and Karim felt anything but normal. They'd developed deeply entrenched, destructive patterns. Stuart began to identify these in a manner that was compassionate and nonjudgmental. Over the first three sessions, they became accustomed to Stuart's consistent leadership in their conversations. Without ever missing a chance, he instructed them to talk more and more about

---

40   S. Johnson and E. Talitman. "Predictors of success in emotionally focused marital therapy." *Journal of Marital and Family Therapy* 23 (1997): 135–152.

what he kept calling the "real" problem—the negative cycle in which they were stuck. Discussing their cycle had an arresting, stabilizing effect on their acute symptoms of distress. In addition to Stephanie and Karim each attending individual therapy sessions once per week, they met for couples therapy twice a week for the first two weeks, then decided to meet once a week after that. In the second week both were sleeping almost normally again, and Stephanie was no longer in a state of total panic. After a month of many therapy sessions, it was time for Stuart to address the cause of the symptoms.

Eventually it became clear to Stephanie and Karim that Stuart was doing more than just labeling what was happening. It was now obvious to them that he was deliberately asking them to focus on certain feelings that were very hard to notice under normal circumstances. Earlier, in the first session, Stuart had surprised Stephanie by bringing attention to her physical state. He had said, "There are two sides to feelings." In particular, he was teaching them to pay attention to one particular side of their feelings, their primary emotions, more than the other side, their secondary emotions.

WHY PRIMARY EMOTIONS ARE
SO IMPORTANT TO EFT

Primary emotions can have either positive or negative tones. They are your "gut level" responses to something you experience, and always affect your body physiologically. Good examples are a pit you feel in your stomach or tension in your shoulders. EFT guides you in how to relax so you can allow yourself to safely experience more of your primary emotions. EFT therapy does not make you more emotional—EFT therapists elicit primary emotions strictly in the service of building emotional intelligence. With greater emotional intelligence, you're more aware of—and in control of—your inner state. That means you're more able to be in sync with those around you.

The most common primary emotions are:

- Fear

- Hurt

- Shame

- Sadness

- Excitement

- Joy

- Surprise

Your primary emotions are your softer side, so to speak, your underbelly. They have the most potential to stimulate active attachment, or bonding, between you and your partner. But you usually don't notice these feelings because of your secondary emotions, or the automatic and instant reactions you have to a primary emotion being triggered.

Typical secondary emotions are:

- Frustration

- Anger

- Numbness

- Guilt

- Defensiveness

Secondary emotions are, in fact, what most people are talking about when they talk about feelings. But these feelings—the reactions you have to your immediate, gut-level, primary feelings—conceal or protect your more vulnerable primary feelings. For example, when Karim said he wanted to "run for the hills" when Stephanie was frustrated with him, he was experiencing a secondary emotion—feeling overwhelmed and wanting relief. Hypothetically, if he was able to interrupt his desire to flee and focus instead on why he was feeling overwhelmed, he might have started to realize it was because he was feeling afraid of being inferior to Stephanie. Fear was his primary feeling. But Karim's adult brain was able to compartmentalize the fear (a primary emotion) and to express something entirely separate, frustration (a secondary emotion), almost instantly. Instead of just feeling helpless in his fear, feeling overwhelmed pushed him into a self-protective, frustrated state.

Most of the arguments and struggles you and your partner have are usually because of the way your secondary emotions ricochet off each other like billiard balls. If you sense your partner's secondary emotion of anger coming on, you're not very likely to want to reveal your vulnerable, primary emotion of hurt or shame. It's just not "safe." You're far more likely to respond to your partner's anger with your own anger, or with avoidance.

The problem with communicating through only secondary emotions is that it creates a circular loop of unproductive attack and withdraw behaviors. *Secondary emotions tend to push others away.* Primary emotions—in moderation—have the potential to connect you with others. The more you express just your frustration (a secondary emotion) without any hint of sadness or hurt, you'll find that your partner may respond with fewer of her own primary emotions and more of her secondary feelings of criticism or attack. Then, you respond with more frustration and anger, and so on. This escalates. Each cycle of this loop removes more and more softness and vulnerability, until all that's left are the hardest, most impenetrable of the secondary emotions—resentment and contempt.

EFT provides you with a way to blend more primary feelings into your communication with your partner, a way to slow down reactive secondary emotions, and a way to build connection and intimacy.

Your EFT therapist will have three goals in mind regarding your negative cycle and primary emotions:

1. Identify and label the steps in your cycle of secondary emotions as a couple, without assigning blame.

2. De-escalate and slow down your cycle when it happens (that is, reduce secondary emotional reactions like defensiveness, criticism, or avoidance) to find primary emotions (vulnerability) that are otherwise obscured by the intense cycling of secondary emotions.

3. Restructure your cycle based on vulnerability while minimizing risk and fostering an atmosphere of experimentation and safety.

Some therapists like to explain and teach these goals and may give you a worksheet to explain or help illustrate your emotional cycle. Others prefer to teach these concepts implicitly, without direct instruction, about the steps along the way.

STEPHANIE AND KARIM BREAK THEIR NEGATIVE CYCLE

One of the unfortunate complications that can arise for couples after an affair is that little attention is given to the primary emotions of the person having the affair. It's easier to empathize with the person who feels betrayed by the infidelity. Experienced professionals should know to look at both parties, however. Partners who feel betrayed do indeed need support and empathy from people who are "totally on their side." However, to fix the problems that created the affair in the first place, a nuanced approach is needed. EFT can work especially well with infidelity because it quickly and consistently addresses the root cause of the affair that's hidden within primary emotions. Once an affair is discovered, most couples take on extremely rigid roles and create an increasingly polarized cycle of negative secondary emotions. That was the case with Stephanie and Karim.

After Stephanie discovered Karim's affair, she and Karim took turns acting out either an aggressively self-justified attitude ("I'm justified to push you, because you pushed me."), or ways of sinking into feelings of defeat and detachment ("You don't matter to me, because I don't matter to you."). Each reaction triggered a disconnection that widened the divide between them—without allowing any deeper primary emotions to propel them toward healing and recovery. When Stephanie was "on the rampage," criticizing Karim for his untrustworthiness, Karim's desire to contact the woman he had been involved with would peak (even though they had since broken things off). And the more tuned-out and "in another world" Karim acted, the more Stephanie's anger and outrage prevailed.

Stephanie often came to sessions feeling "like a loaded gun," with an exhaustive list of questions she had about Karim's affair. She told Stuart that these episodes had occurred a few times a week. Stuart asked Stephanie if she could trust him to ask Karim some questions about the affair on her behalf. She was happy to surrender her typical role of managing what was happening, because trying to compel Karim to be trustworthy took a tremendous amount of energy from her.

"I feel so depressed after I pursue him for details about the affair," she said.

Karim and Stephanie attended weekly EFT sessions with Stuart for ten weeks straight. When friends asked them how the therapy was going, they couldn't always explain. But their wildly fluctuating feelings about each other began to steady as the sessions progressed. The pair both felt as though they were making progress, and trusted that they were in the right kind of therapy. In their tenth session, they had a particularly big breakthrough about the affair.

"Stephanie," Stuart started, "before I ask Karim about the affair, I want to say that what you just told me about your feeling depressed is really amazing."

"It is?" Stephanie shot back quizzically. "It doesn't feel amazing."

"I know," said Stuart. "But you're basically telling me 'I just want to explode at you for doing this to me, because you mean so much to me. In fact, you mean so much to me that I'm totally wiped out. I'm depressed and empty without you.'"

"Yeah…that's exactly it," Stephanie stammered. "I, well, I never put it that way before."

Stuart, trained to see the attachment needs underneath hard-to-relate-to behavior like rage, had zeroed in on Stephanie's admission of her soft spot—her depression—underneath her secondary emotion of anger. He was quick to put her vulnerability in a positive light, since most couples at this stage of disengagement have learned to associate vulnerability with not getting what they need. But in EFT, as with the other attachment-based therapies in this book, vulnerability is redeemed. Couples are taught to see it as a key that can open the door to the possibility of safely asking for and getting what you need the most in your relationship.

Stuart looked at Stephanie. He could sense that although her anger was hurtful to Karim, deep inside it was an innocent protest against losing someone she loved. Her eyes were already telling him he'd struck a chord. Looking back at Stuart with softness, she then quickly scanned Karim as if to see if he would notice the stirrings of tenderness toward him, and reach for her. Turning now to Karim, Stuart said he wondered if Karim could see what he was seeing in Stephanie's eyes. Karim confirmed with a slight nod and the raise of an eyebrow. Stuart asked him what happened inside of him when she looked at him that way.

When EFT therapists want to evoke your vulnerable primary emotions, it's typical for them to ask, "What happens inside of you when...?" You won't hear many questions that start with "What do you think...?" because they don't want you to respond by thinking analytically all the time. EFT therapists believe that thinking is a secondary-level neurological event. Stuart knew that Stephanie was taking a big risk by letting herself remain soft and open while waiting for Karim to answer, despite the many reasons she had to stiffen up and turn away. Stuart wanted Karim to answer not from his head but from his heart. For the first time, he could tell that Stephanie was ready to meet him with her own, more open, heart.

"Well," Karim started, taking a moment to notice his physical reaction and *all* his feelings, not just the first thought that came to his mind. "I honestly feel like raw hamburger. I want to crawl under a rock." His normally solid frame hunched forward a bit, head and eyes turned down. His body language said he was emotionally exhausted, too. He looked sad.

"Whoa," replied Stuart, visibly moved by such a powerfully fragile display. In the negative cycle with Stephanie, Karim typically mentioned needing more space, so crawling under a rock was not a new sentiment. But he usually couched it as a secondary emotion—he would feel defensive and ask for more space to avoid having to confront the uncomfortable feelings that otherwise emerged. This was the first time he'd linked his primary emotion (feeling hurt, like "raw hamburger") with his secondary emotion, feeling defensive ("I want to crawl under a rock"), and let his vulnerability surface outwardly. Instead of just pushing Stephanie away with his withdrawal, he was tentative and even balking about his need to retreat. Stuart had clearly helped make an opening for this to occur by slowing Stephanie down. Now, he wondered, could they hold the course and take a tentative step toward each other?

Stuart moved decisively to solidify the potential for connection that was starting to take place between Stephanie and Karim. "I get it, and really appreciate how much you're saying by putting that out there," Stuart said. "Can you tell Stephanie more about the raw hamburger part? I'm sensing that Stephanie's 'gun' is kind of unloaded now." He looked up to check in with Stephanie. He was right. Her countenance showed the same tenderness as it had a moment ago, and as she met Karim's eyes she gave a slight, reassuring nod.

Karim fidgeted as Stephanie held his gaze. He was uncomfortable even looking directly at her. It had been a long time since he'd truly felt that Stephanie was disarmed, but he would later say this was the moment when he knew it would be impossible to cheat on her again. He referred to this moment as finding his "kryptonite" for the affair, because it felt so good to truly know again that she wanted him—that she believed in him and that he could really make her happy.

After what seemed like a long time, he quietly reached for Stephanie's hand.

"I only cheated—" he cut himself off, closing his eyes to collect himself, to let his usual feeling of resentment and anger move within him before reacting. He hated being unfaithful, and was flooded by resentment and shame for being in a position where cheating felt like a good option. But several sessions of EFT had taught him to notice his feelings more carefully—and to not be afraid of feeling them. Doing so gave him more command of his reactions. As he welcomed his anger with curiosity instead of hostility (anger at being angry), he relaxed slightly and could also feel other feelings mixed in with the anger.

"Stay with it," coached Stuart. "Stay with the feeling underneath the anger."

Karim's face went through what seemed like tortured contortions until the dam broke. He finally leaned over to Stephanie and looked at her, tears streaking down his face. He spoke longingly about his desire to be fully "there" for her.

"Cheating was nothing for me," he said. "I never want to do it again, and you don't deserve that. You mean everything, absolutely everything to me…"

Stephanie could feel a compassion and connection to Karim that went beyond forgiveness. It would take her a long time to truly forgive and sort out her confusion after being deceived, but absolute forgiveness wasn't necessary to love and feel loved. That's what she wanted the most. She felt an intense connection to Karim, and she pulled him into a full embrace.

This breakthrough started to make daily life much easier, but Stephanie and Karim continued in EFT therapy for six more months. Like most couples who enter therapy in as much distress as they had, they couldn't easily access primary emotions. But each time they showed up to see Stuart, as Stephanie put it, "something good always happened." It was a high compliment from someone who'd been almost ready to drop her husband off at the therapist's doorstep and call her lawyer.

IS EMOTIONALLY FOCUSED COUPLES THERAPY OUR STYLE?

Do you want to know if EFT is for you? Take a look at this summary of the features of EFT that differentiate it from other types of therapy. Keep in mind that some therapists use EFT techniques all the time, while others may use them only when the techniques are the best choice. It's critical that you ask your therapist how closely he or she adheres to the "pure" EFT model, if that's important to you.

EFT is unique because:

- It aims to create a secure attachment to your partner by teaching you to become more comfortable with certain emotions—ones that make you feel vulnerable or playful—and to use those emotions to heal and grow more connected to each other.

- It's a couples therapy that uses methods validated by research. This means that studies have been conducted in such a way that demonstrates positive outcomes with couples as a result of EFT methods. It's rare for psychotherapy to have empirical validation. By comparison, Imago and Gottman couples therapies are still in the process of conducting successful validation studies.

- EFT doesn't make you more emotional, it increases emotional intelligence. One study showed that this method works especially well for men who are considered by their wives to be "emotionally inexpressive."

- Couples who have been through EFT report an increase in their ability to solve problems together, even though problem-solving is not the main focus of therapy.

FITTING-ROOM QUIZ

Answer these questions to see if Emotionally Focused Therapy for Couples might be a good fit for you and your partner:

A. I want a therapist who's going to teach me emotional intelligence—how to respond to emotions I'm feeling in a way that's useful—by showing me how to attune to subtle sensations in my body and mind.

1. I could use all the emotional intelligence instruction I can get. Sign me up!

2. I like the idea of focusing on emotions, and I'd also be interested in getting advice that's concrete and actionable.

3. If it's good for me, I'll go along with the program, but focusing on feelings is not my first or second choice.

4. No way! "Attuning to sensations in my body" sounds like psychobabble mumbo-jumbo.

B. **It's important to me that the couples therapy I'm in is validated by research that shows it's effective.**

1. Absolutely. There's no room for guessing about what works and what doesn't.

2. This sounds important. I'm definitely intrigued.

3. Research-based information is nice but not the most important part of couples therapy to me.

4. It's more important to find a therapist who clicks with us than one who uses the "right" methods.

C. **How comfortable are you with this statement: "The strongest among us are those who can reach for others. Love is the best survival strategy of all."**

1. We all need each other. Love is the answer!

2. I believe in love, and I also enjoy having "space in our togetherness."

3. I believe in love, and I believe in it even more when it's not breathing down my neck.

4. Self-sufficiency comes first, then, if there's any extra room, love can come along for the ride.

D. Do you want solutions and an actionable strategy for fixing your relationship or are you comfortable with a better relationship without necessarily being able to explain how it all happened?

1. I want a great relationship first and foremost…how we get there isn't important to me.

2. I don't need to be able to explain everything, the strategies will fall into place.

3. I prefer to have lots of concrete instructions in therapy, but will go with the flow if it works out for the best

4. What's the point of going to therapy if we don't always know precisely how it's helping us?

E. To create emotional safety in therapy sessions, EFT therapists are trained to "take the bullet" for one partner when the other is criticizing or attacking. The strategy is to divert attention away from the intended target until safer, primary emotions can be communicated. How would this feel to you?

1. As far as I'm concerned, my therapist can take *all* the bullets for me. I need my therapist on my side when I'm under attack!

2. This sure would be nice to have support when I need it, but I don't want training wheels on all the time.

3. Most of the time I don't think this is necessary, but it would be nice to have occasional referee intervention when things get really heated.

4. This would drive me crazy! How can we be real with each other if our therapist constantly interferes?

How to Score Your Answers

Add the numbers you chose for your answers, and then use the chart below to determine what kind of match Emotionally Focused Therapy for couples is for you. Do the same for your partner's score, and use the fit rating to further assess your compatibility with this brand of therapy.

Just Right: If your total is 5–10, it's a great fit, and you'll likely be intrigued by EFT. Strongly consider finding a therapist who uses this kind of therapy.

Loose Fit: If your total is 11–15, it's a decent fit, but some aspects of EFT methods may not thrill you. You might want to look into Imago and possibly compare with an alternative to be sure.

Tight Squeeze: If your total is 16–20, you could be more annoyed by than receptive to EFT methods. Proceed with caution, and interview potential therapists carefully. Feel free to work with an EFT therapist if he or she uses these methods judiciously and perhaps in combination with other methods that are a better fit for you—perhaps from either Imago Relationship Therapy or the Gottman Method Couples Therapy.

Keep in mind that this "fit-ness" test is a very rough guide. Just like clothing sizes vary between manufacturers, you could find wide variation between any two EFT therapists. Depending on the therapist's exposure to other significant couples therapy training, he or she may depend exclusively on using EFT methods or use it only when it's a good fit.

FURTHER READING

Johnson, Susan M. 2008. *Hold me tight: seven conversations for a lifetime of love.* New York: Little, Brown & Co.

Johnson, Susan M. 2013. *Love sense.* New York: Hachette, Little, Brown and Company.

PART III
SOME ASSEMBLY REQUIRED

CHAPTER 7
HOW MUCH DOES COUPLES THERAPY COST?

"A surgeon announces his retirement at age fifty-five. His amazed and envious colleagues ask him how he can do it. 'Simple,' he answers with a smile. 'One wife, one house.'"

—Anonymous

YOU AND YOUR partner are finally ready to meet with a couples therapist. Congratulations. According to research, the average couple spends approximately six years being unhappy before calling someone for help.[41] Hopefully, you haven't waited that long. But if you've waited a long time, don't despair. It's never too late to try to turn things around.

Now that you're going to go to couples therapy, you might

---

41   Notarius, C., & Buongiorno, J. (1992). Wait time until professional treatment in marital therapy. Unpublished paper, Catholic University of America, Washington, DC.

be wondering how much it will cost, why couples therapy tends to be more expensive than alternatives like self-help or educational programs, and whether there are any free services for couples counseling—and, if so, whether they're any good.

THE BOTTOM LINE: INVEST IN YOUR MARRIAGE

The joke opening this chapter illustrates a simple point: There are tangible, monetary benefits to avoiding divorce. For that reason alone, couples therapy—done right—is worth considering as a solid investment. According to Forbes.com, the average cost of a contested divorce is about $15,000.[42] This doesn't factor in the cost of new housing or moving expenses, nor does it include the cost of family counseling for any children involved.

As we've seen, you have many choices for the type of couples therapy you might put your time and money toward. Once you're confident in the couples therapy you've chosen, it's up to you to protect this investment by becoming as knowledgeable as you can about how it works. You're the most invested party, in more ways than one. If you do your homework, you have a better shot at finding the best therapist and getting the most out of the dollars you invest. Couples therapy is a big-ticket investment in your family's wellness, but it can yield some big-ticket returns.

---

42 http://www.forbes.com/sites/jefflanders/2013/09/10/two-divorce-trends-identified-in-the-legal-marketplace/

THE HONEST COST OF MARRIAGE COUNSELING

I can't tell you how much *your* marriage counseling is going to cost any more than I can tell you how long you might have to wait in a hospital emergency room before you receive treatment. But I *can* discuss the many variables that affect the cost of couples therapy, which include setting clear goals and selecting the right therapist for you and your partner, as well as using health insurance, selecting the frequency of sessions, and analyzing the severity of mental health issues in your relationship.

If you have a relatively healthy marriage, therapy will cost less than if you're living out the film *The War of the Roses.* In that dark comedy, Michael Douglas and Kathleen Turner are embroiled in a bitter divorce, fighting for each and every possession. In the end, their divorce costs them everything, including their lives. This is a melodramatic example, but you get my point. Divorce is costly to one's finances as well as emotional stability and dreams.

At the time of this printing, the typical price for counseling runs anywhere between $100-$300 per session. Each session will run from forty-five to eighty or ninety minutes in length. The longer your sessions, the higher your bill. Some marriage counselors insist on meeting for longer than sixty minutes, others insist that anything longer than sixty minutes is too long. Also, having two people in a session simply requires more time. However, there are still situations where shorter meetings may be indicated as a best practice. For example, if hostility cannot be addressed and contained in a session in a way that creates a productive meeting, shorter sessions may be suggested—in addition to private counseling sessions between your conjoint meetings.

If your relationship is in moderate distress, the recommended frequency of couples counseling sessions is typically once per week. If your relationship is in severe distress (high levels of contempt, hopelessness, distance, and isolation), it's not uncommon to undertake weekly couples sessions plus adjunct individual therapy for both parties, which may also be once per week. So if your relationship is in serious trouble, you could be looking at a price tag of between $350-$600 per week (for all three sessions combined). Most couples spend much less than this—between $75–250 per week (or much less if you're able to work with a therapist inside your insurance network)—and still receive excellent results in the hands of an experienced couples therapist.

WHY COUPLES THERAPY CAN BE SO EXPENSIVE

The overall cost of couples therapy, start to finish, increases proportionate to factors such as whether you have significant mental health or substance abuse issues, if you are also seeing an individual therapist who gives you advice that runs counter to what you hear in couples therapy, or if you encounter logistical interference that prevents you from attending regular and frequent sessions. Therapists' fees in cities are usually higher than those in rural areas.

- **Mental health, substance abuse, or infidelity issues:** When there are clear individual mental health symptoms in one or both partners—like depression, an anxiety disorder, an active addiction, or infidelity—many counselors will recommend that each partner undergo therapy with an individual therapist in addition to (or before) beginning couples sessions. Some couples therapists won't work with you if there's active infidelity or addiction, but others do. Across the board, it's a best practice for a therapist to refer you to a specialist when necessary, and specialists can be more expensive.

- **Working with an individual therapist or couples therapist who undermines your relationship:** In Chapter 4, we saw how some types of therapy can actually be hazardous to your relationship. I'm very careful to refer my clients for individual therapy only to a therapist trained in relational psychology—the idea that our thoughts, feelings, and behavior are created by our relationships, not merely hard-wired personality traits. Such specialized therapists understand that anything that affects our relationships also affects our thoughts, feelings, and behavior. For example, if your therapist believes codependency—relying on your partner to meet your emotional needs—is unhealthy in any struggling relationship, he or she is likely to emphasize individual responsibility over mutual responsibility to improve your relationship. Consider finding a therapist who has the skills and training to help you create a shared sense of responsibility for your relationship and who is open to fostering healthy levels of individual autonomy (see Chapter 3).

- **Scheduling problems with you or your therapist:** Make sure the therapist you choose is available to meet with you consistently. Ideally, try to set regular weekly meeting times. You don't want to start making progress only to have your therapist say she can't see you again for another two months because she's disappearing to the South of France. It's also less economically productive if you or your partner miss multiple weeks of therapy because of your own scheduling issues.

- **Geographical convenience:** It may be convenient for you to walk ten minutes from your office to your therapist's office, but a therapist whose office is located in a downtown area pays a much higher rent and thus has higher overhead cost—that cost gets passed on to you. You're more likely to find a lower-priced therapist in a location that isn't easily accessible by public transit and that's located in a less-affluent zip code. Of course, you need to also consider that a practice's good reputation will command higher fees.

HOW TO STAY OUT OF THE
COUPLES THERAPY MONEY PIT

Taking an active role in choosing the right therapist for you, setting goals, and voicing feedback during therapy will influence how you view the success of your therapy. Without approaching therapy in a structured way, it can become a "money pit," a quagmire of inadequate results and over-budget expenses. It's important to find a therapist with whom you and your partner truly resonate, to determine the optimal frequency of your sessions, and to begin to assess whether any progress is being made after a few sessions.

According to significant research about how clients view the outcomes of therapy, the biggest factor affecting success is client involvement and client belief in therapy.[43] To believe in the therapy, you need a basic understanding of what's possible and you need to know what's expected of you. I wrote this book to help you make an informed decision. When you read Part II of this book, you learned about the Big Three brands of couples therapy. You can use your knowledge of these major brands to find a therapist who resonates the most with you—even if the therapist doesn't subscribe dogmatically to one of the Big Three methods in particular. Interview therapists to see if they deliver some aspect of the method that most appealed to you.

I strongly suggest that you interview your therapist on the phone, and then schedule your first meeting only if you feel comfortable with how your initial questions are answered. Some therapists offer a free twenty-minute consultation. In many cases, my practice offers an in-person, twenty-minute free consultation in addition to any initial phone conversation; we know what a serious investment it is to find the right therapist to work with.

If you like the way the first session is conducted, consider scheduling a series of three or four appointments on the spot.

---

43   Cited in *The Heart and Soul of Change, Second Edition: Delivering What Works in Therapy*, 2010. Edited by Barry L. Duncan, PsyD; Scott D. Miller, PhD; Bruce E. Wampold, PhD; and Mark A. Hubble, PhD.

Don't wait around and think about it or solicit advice from friends—trust your own instincts about what's right for you. To believe in your therapy and get the best outcome, nurture and protect your investment and the feelings you have toward therapy.

After you've met with your therapist a few times, assess how much progress you've made. Ask yourself, "Is this what I was expecting?" If not, don't be shy about asking the therapist to make adjustments in how you're working together. Voice your concerns. You'll get your money's worth if you take an active role in your therapy. Good therapists respect your vocal participation—great ones love it. You're testing your therapist's bona fides a bit. I'm not saying you should challenge your therapist just for the heck of it, but by all means don't keep quiet about any real concerns you have. If you do, I guarantee you won't feel as though you got your money's worth.

HOW TO SET GOALS TO KNOW WHEN YOU'RE DONE WITH THERAPY

When you first meet with your therapist, tell him or her what you hope to accomplish. This is the best way to avoid spending money on therapy that isn't productive for your relationship. The seven most common goals I've heard from couples visiting my practice are:

- To improve communication

- To be able to trust each other more

- To reduce hostility and find better ways to express disagreement

- To parent as a team

- To feel closer to each other

- To assess if the relationship is worth trying to save

- To overcome stale intimacy and create more passion

If one of your goals is to feel closer to each other as a result of couples therapy, ask yourself, "In eight weeks, how would I know if I'm feeling closer to my partner?" If you aren't sure how you'd know if you've met that goal, try to use a common goal-setting exercise that will help you define a "S.M.A.R.T" goal (see below).

SET S.M.A.R.T GOALS FOR YOUR COUPLES THERAPY

S.M.A.R.T is an acronym that stands for:

Specific: The What, Why, and How

Measurable: How much? How many? How will I know when it is accomplished?

Attainable: Are you prepared to do the work needed to make this goal happen? If not, is there a more attainable goal that you're ready to tackle?

Relevant: Is your goal consistent with other goals and values you have?

Time-based: Set a start time and target deadline for your goal.

Here's an example of how you might assess the goal of feeling closer to your partner, according to the S.M.A.R.T. matrix:

- **Specific:** Feeling closer means different things to both of us. We want help having conversations about what our differences mean in a productive, clear, and respectful way.

- **Measurable:** I want my partner and I to be able to express the importance of closeness without being defensive or disrespectful of the other's point of view. This could be measured by any third party observing us who would notice if we show respect for each other's attempts at connection. (Do we roll our eyes at each other when we're upset? Do we acknowledge points of view different from our own?)

- **Attainable:** Neither one of us finds the goal of being closer to each other to be unrealistic. We both agree that feeling close is important and are ready to be challenged to improve this. Neither one of us will expect the other to completely agree with one single definition of what it means to feel close.

- **Relevant:** We both see the value in finding ways to be agreeable about how to be close to each other in ways that work for both of us.

- **Time-based:** We're not expecting to feel close to each other twenty-four hours a day, seven days a week. A time-limited goal would be that, over the course of a week, each of us will feel close to the other around 50 percent of the time. We'll start keeping track in week two of therapy and expect to see improvement each week, reaching 50 percent by no later than week eight of therapy.

Setting a S.M.A.R.T goal for your therapy requires that you define your goal as something specific, measurable, attainable, realistic, and time-based. The best way to avoid going over budget and making more visits than necessary to a couples therapist is to set realistic goals at the very beginning of therapy. Assess your progress regularly with each other and with your therapist.

HOW TO FIND QUALITY COUPLES THERAPY FOR FREE

Universities and teaching hospitals often run public clinics where students who are studying counseling or psychiatry may provide their services for free or reduced rates. These students receive clinical supervision while working with clients. Some of these centers have excellent reputations. Well-regarded teachers and staff may also offer their services pro bono, based on economic need or your participation in research. For example, one woman told me that even though she knew the student counselor working with her was inexperienced, she also knew that counselor met weekly with several well-known, talented clinicians who gave her feedback and guidance. The woman told me she loved the idea that there were so many people thinking about her situation, trying to help her. Some people have had wonderful experiences at training clinics. However, results may vary.

Community mental health clinics/agencies in most cities provide free psychiatric services for individuals diagnosed with a significant mental health condition (Axis I diagnosis). These services tend to focus more on treating severe mental illness and provide social work services to assist with substance abuse treatment, housing, employment, and medical care. Once enrolled in services with a community mental health agency, individual or couples counseling may be an option.

Churches, synagogues, and mosques often promote family and marriage classes and may offer private meetings with clergy for relationship advice. Most clergy who refer clients to our practice tell me that they're comfortable counseling couples going through "a few bumps." Some clergy are well suited to offer pragmatic advice and guidance to couples along with their spiritual and religious teaching. Most members of the clergy refer highly symptomatic couples to the more specialized care of a couples therapist. However, more and more seminaries are offering courses in marriage and family care, and you may find a person highly trained or experienced in family care on staff in larger congregations or parishes.

Don't be afraid to ask your clergy member about his or her training, and how it compares to that of a clinical couples therapist. If you meet with your clergy, be just as direct as you would with a therapist: ask about goals and the type of interventions that you can expect. Most clergy and religious leaders provide spiritual insight based on religious teachings about marriage or love. For some couples, this kind of spiritual encouragement is all that's needed or it forms an important component of getting help. If you suspect you need more specialized help than what your clergy can provide, ask him or her for referrals to professional resources in your community.

Even in major cities, where the cost of therapy is higher, some therapists may offer lower fees depending on a client's situation. Few will advertise this. Some might base their fees on your income, for example. It never hurts to ask and to try to find someone who is willing to work with you at a reduced rate.

HOW TO USE YOUR INSURANCE BENEFITS TO GET EXCELLENT COUPLES THERAPY

When you begin to investigate whether your insurance company will cover part of the cost of couples therapy, don't ask "Do you cover marriage counseling or couples counseling?" The answer will almost always be "No." Phrase it this way: "Do I have any coverage for conjoint psychotherapy?"

Maybe somewhere out there an insurance agent is reading this and will correct me, but I don't think insurance companies allow their staff to tell you—unless you ask specifically—that couples counseling is covered under conjoint psychotherapy. It's my belief that failing to elaborate about how couples therapy is covered by insurance is a tactic used by managed health care organizations to reduce the number of claims made. This tactic should be a crime. But since it's not, you have to know the right questions to ask. And for the record, couples therapy is technically a health care benefit.

The next question that you need to be sure to ask is whether your health insurance provides in-network coverage, out-of-network coverage, or both. In-network benefits are those health services (including psychotherapy) that are paid for directly by your insurance. When using in-network benefits, you usually only pay a small copay ($10-$30) out of pocket at each visit. Your doctor or therapist submits the insurance claim, and you do no other paperwork except to give the provider your insurance information at your first visit. An out-of-network benefit is one in which your plan pays for doctor or therapist visits partially or in full, but you have to submit the insurance claim yourself and pay the provider up front. A doctor or therapist who does not accept insurance is called a fee-for-service provider.

When you call your insurance company to inquire about the extent of your psychotherapy coverage, including conjoint psychotherapy, you need to be prepared to provide a current procedural terminology (CPT) code to describe the exact service for which you're seeking coverage. The CPT code is usually listed on your invoice, but you can always call your therapist to ask which CPT codes he or she uses. In Appendix C, "Questions to Ask Your Insurance Company," I've given you a worksheet to use to help you ask the right questions when inquiring about your insurance benefit for therapy.

You're likely to encounter another frustrating idiosyncrasy about dealing with insurance companies: insurance companies often won't tell you how much they'll pay for each code until *after* you submit a claim. The first time I encountered this "secret coverage provision" with my own insurance company, I almost asked, "Is this a joke?" I assure you it wasn't. Getting the CPT code runaround was like going to the bank to ask for the balance in your account but being told you had to write a check before they'd tell you what was in your account.

If you have a paid provider organization (PPO) or a point of service (POS) insurance plan, you're usually eligible for considerable out-of-pocket reimbursement for both couples and individual psychotherapy. To get these reimbursements, you usually have to submit an insurance claim yourself and pay the provider up front. Some psychotherapy practices may submit out-of-network claims for you and the reimbursement check will be mailed to you.

Why is knowing your reimbursement eligibility important? Because, unlike medical providers (physicians), a growing majority of mental health providers (psychotherapists) are not in-network providers for insurance companies. Many psychotherapists are strictly fee-for-service providers, meaning that they only accept direct payment from you at the time of service and don't accept insurance. If you have a PPO or POS plan (plans that reimburse for fee-for-service expenses), call the number on the back of your insurance card to inquire about your out-of-network benefits. Find out the amount of your deductible—the amount you have to pay each calendar year before health insurance kicks in a reimbursement to you. Once you've paid your deductible, the reimbursement is often between 40 to 60 percent of the "allowed" fees, the maximum amount the insurance company will reimburse for a particular service.

Insurance companies allow higher reimbursements for providers with different professional degrees. Your insurance reimbursement will likely be higher for professionals who have credentials that are deemed by the insurance company to be worth a higher rate. Mental health professionals are lumped into one of two possible fee groups: the lower-rate group consists of Licensed Professional Counselors, Licensed Marriage and Family Therapists, and Social Workers; the higher-rate group consists of Psychologists, Psychiatric Nurses, and Psychiatrists.

People call our practice every day who don't realize that, for just a little bit of legwork on their part, they could be seeing an excellent out-of-network counselor and taking advantage of often substantial reimbursement from their insurance. As I explain in more detail below, in some parts of the country, out-of-network therapists deliver a much higher quality of service as compared to their in-network counterparts. This is due in part to the increased level of attention that out-of-network providers usually give to you. They are being paid roughly 60 percent more than they would earn from being an in-network provider. In my experience, out-of-network providers are more highly trained, more clinically efficient, and have more time to take care of themselves to avoid professional burnout.

Once you learn the steps necessary to submit your own insurance claim, the reimbursement process is usually pretty straightforward. The insurance provider mails a check to you anywhere from two to three weeks after you submit the claim. Some companies let you submit a claim online, while others ask you to fax or mail in a hard copy of your invoice.

One health insurance provider recently published a chart on its website similar to the one below, which explains how its out-of-network behavioral health reimbursement works.

Type of visit example: 30-minute psychotherapy session

	Psychiatrist	Psychologist	Social Worker
Your provider's bill	$200	$200	$200
Our "allowed" or "recognized" amount for this type of professional	$140	$110	$85
Plan payment (65 percent of our "allowed" amount)	$91	$71	$55
Your total out-of-pocket cost	$109	$129	$145
Your deductible	$0	$0	$0
Your coinsurance (30 percent of the allowed amount)	$42	$33	$26
Additional balance billed by your provider	$60	$96	$119

You can look up the cost of a particular procedure (CPT) code for your city or state on the American Medical Association (AMA) website.[44] The AMA website also gives the current Medicaid reimbursement amount for various CPT codes. Your private insurance reimbursement will be different from the Medicaid reimbursement, but most are based on the Medicaid rate, so you can at least see the relative scale of one code compared to another.

GETTING THE PROCEDURE CODE RIGHT

If you're meeting with a therapist for couples counseling, the procedure code that's often used is 90847, which designates conjoint psychotherapy. The reimbursement rate for this code may not be dependent on how long your sessions are—a 45-minute 90847 may reimburse the same amount as a 90-minute 90847, for example. However, if you do meet with a therapist for individual sessions, there are two CPT coding options your therapist could use on your invoices that might make a significant difference in the amount you're eligible to receive as a reimbursement.

Some clients have reported to me that if a therapist can meet for sixty minutes (code 90837) rather than the standard forty-five (code 90834), they'll get a better reimbursement. By meeting for the extra fifteen minutes and using the corresponding code, their reimbursement percentage increased from 43 percent to 51 percent (a net gain of 8 percent).[45] Their session time increased by 33 percent, however, with only a 15 percent increase in out-

---

44   www.ama-assn.org

45   These illustrations are only hypothetical and subject to wide variation, depending on your specific out-of-network insurance plan and regional differences between insurance providers. Be sure to check with your therapist and insurance plan to learn about your situation.

of-pocket cost—that evens out to a 14 percent decrease in the dollar per minute, out-of-pocket rate.

The rules your therapist must follow when choosing the correct CPT code for your situation may vary from state to state. It's also a matter of individual preference for some therapists and you'll find wide variation in how receptive some therapists are to your input about how the CPT code is chosen.

Here's an example with rates based on an industry approximation (as of publication). The bottom three rows illustrate the percentages discussed above.

	45 minutes (908.34)	60 minutes (908.37)	Variance in $	Variance in %
Cost of session	$150	$200	$50	—
Reimbursement percentage	43%	51%	—	8%
Reimbursement total	$65	$102	$37	—
Net out-of-pocket cost	**$85**	**$98**	**$13**	**15%**
Session minutes	**45**	**60**	**—**	**33%**
Out-of-pocket dollar per minute	**$1.89**	**$1.63**	**-$.26**	**-14%**

COMMON CPT CODES USED
FOR PSYCHOTHERAPY

You might receive invoices from your therapist with CPT codes that you can't decipher. The following are the most commonly used procedure codes used for insurance reimbursement of psychotherapy. This includes the code 90847, often used for conjoint sessions (counseling with more than one person).

90791 Initial Evaluation

90832 Psychotherapy, 30 minutes with patient and/or family member

90834 Psychotherapy, 45 minutes with patient and/or family member

90837 Psychotherapy, 60 minutes with patient and/or family member

90845 Psychoanalysis

90846 Family psychotherapy without the patient present

90847 Family psychotherapy, conjoint psychotherapy with the patient present

90849 Multiple-family group psychotherapy

90853 Group psychotherapy (other than of a multiple-family group)

Above, you'll notice that the more impersonal term "patient" is used. Insurance companies (as well as many psychoanalysts or psychiatrists) still use the term "patient," while most other therapists refer to the person receiving therapy as a "client."

INSURANCE AND YOUR PRIVACY

Keep in mind that when you attend family or conjoint psychotherapy, the therapist isn't usually required to report to the insurance company who else attended the session besides the person identified as the patient on the claim. For members of the military or government officials concerned about your name being "on record" with a mental health professional, know that your attendance likely won't be shared with the insurance company if your name isn't on the bill. Of course, you'll want to check with your insurance provider for verification.

Normal limits of the confidentiality of your therapist's records include instances where your therapist is a "mandated reporter" of imminent harm to yourself or others, or circumstances where reporting the abuse of children is legally required. Some government or military security clearance requirements stipulate that the applicant consents to the review of health records.

Your therapy invoice is also likely to only list one name, even if two of you attended conjoint therapy sessions. This is because most insurance companies require one name per claim. If your husband puts his name on the invoice you cannot submit an invoice with your name for the same service. Choosing which of your names goes on your invoice may not matter much to you. However, be sure to discuss this with your partner in advance if you have concerns about your name being identified in your insurance file as the recipient of mental health services. If you don't plan to submit your invoice for an insurance claim, your therapist should be able to list both you and your partner's name on your invoice.

GETTING A DIAGNOSIS CODE
YOU CAN LIVE WITH

One item you'll likely see on an invoice from your therapist is a diagnosis code. The diagnosis code is one of the most personal pieces of information that could be shared with a third party, but insurance companies require it.[46] An insurance company will occasionally request details about your therapy to authorize reimbursement, but this is rare in most cases except for in-network claims or for claims related to substance-abuse treatment. It's atypical for an insurance company to require specific information about the nature of your treatment for out-of-network claims, but a so-called "utilization review" by the insurance company could ask your therapist to provide a diagnosis and a summary of your treatment plan.

One of the most commonly used diagnosis codes in most therapy practices is 309.9, which is Adjustment Disorder, Non-specified. This relatively innocuous "disorder" basically means that you're experiencing stress from a life challenge. I don't know about you, but there isn't a single day that goes by for me that wouldn't fall under this description. Bottom line: if you're worried that a diagnostic label your therapist gives you on your insurance claim could haunt you later (when

---

46   If you're not submitting an insurance claim, your therapist may be willing to provide services without using a formal mental health diagnosis.

you're applying for a security clearance for example) discuss this with your prospective therapist.[47]

HOW TO FIND A GOOD COUPLES THERAPIST USING HMO BENEFITS

Health maintenance organization (HMO) insurance plans don't have an out-of-network provision for reimbursement, which means only health providers listed in the HMO network are covered. So how do you find a good couples therapist if you have an HMO?

First, let's address the quality of therapy services available in-network versus the quality of therapy services available out-of-network. Ask ten psychotherapists their opinion about practicing inside or outside of an insurance network, and you'll get ten different responses. Some therapists feel strongly that they're ethically obligated to provide service to people bound to use an HMO for behavioral health care. Others feel strongly that they're ethically compelled to resist the trend of insurance companies severely undervaluing and underpaying behavioral health workers. Of the therapists who won't participate in an HMO (or any insurance at all), they cite the fact that even the best fees that insurance companies pay a therapist only amount to roughly 60 percent of what a therapist could earn by charging clients directly for services.

---

47   Many couples therapists have clear, written policies that state they will not willingly provide information about your couples therapy treatment to any attorney you or your partner may use in future divorce or custody proceedings.

Some of these out-of-network therapists therefore say there are no "good" therapists on insurance panels—the network of clinicians available to insurance members. That follows from two general, related ideas. First is the idea that less talented or less experienced therapists wouldn't be able to maintain a private practice and must rely on insurance referrals to stay in business. The second is that many therapists—couples therapists perhaps chief among them—are specialists who have invested significantly in post-graduate training and certifications. Keep in mind these beliefs are generalizations, but they reflect opinions of many colleagues I've encountered over the years.

If you're going to use your in-network benefits for counseling, an upside is that you'll only have to pay a small copay of $10 or $20. This sounds like a fantastic deal, but it usually correlates to therapists with less experience or competence. Nevertheless, use the extremely low out-of-pocket fees associated with in-network psychotherapists to your advantage if you must. Shop around like crazy. Visit as many therapists as it takes to find the gem who is competent and experienced and will help you and your relationship the most. I can assure you that, despite the widespread belief that out-of-network therapists are better, there are many exceptions.[48]

Consider also that rates of reimbursement for mental health services have not increased in twenty years, and have sometimes actually *declined*. Despite the mental health parity

---

48   Some parts of the country seem especially prone to experience the "brain-drain" of therapists from insurance panels, while in other parts of the country almost every therapist is affiliated with an insurance company. Differences among regional insurance reimbursement rates likely play a role in how many clinicians remain on a given insurance panel.

act passed in 2008, the fact is that health insurance pays substantially less for mental health care than for medical care. According to Dr. Ivan J. Miller, a mental health care advocate, only 44 percent of health insurance premiums reach mental health care practitioners, verses 80 percent for medical practitioners. This practice, known as cost-shifting, deliberately underfunds psychiatric care in order to pay for the physical health care costs associated with operating physical-care hospitals.[49]

Earlier in the book, in Chapter 3, I discussed why I think attachment-based approaches are an essential part of effective couples therapy. Now that you have a sense of what to expect in this type of therapy, you know more about what to look for—even if you decide attachment-based therapies aren't for you. If you're using your in-network insurance benefits, take advantage of the lower fees for each session by simply having more sessions. I suggest using your first session like an interview—get to know the background of your therapist. Discuss how well he or she understands new methods of couples therapy that use attachment-based methods, and how she thinks this differs from traditional, behavioral-based couples therapies. Use the "Ten Questions to Ask When Searching for a Couples Counselor" in Chapter 10 to ensure that your therapist will use a style of therapy that is most compatible with your needs.

Despite the unevenness of mental health care available via

---

49   Ivan J. Miller, "Hardball with Managed Care: Enforcing a *Real* Parity Law." *The Independent Practitioner 25(3).* (2005): 133–135. http://www. ivanjmiller.com/index.html.

health insurance, and the "brain-drain" of some of the best psychotherapists, who leave HMO networks to practice exclusively out-of-network, you don't need to despair if you can't go outside your insurance network to find a therapist. Be willing to do a little extra research and to spend more time finding a therapist who has invested in supervision and training to compensate for a limited choice among providers. You *can* find dedicated professionals working within the managed care or Medicaid network of therapists.

CHAPTER 8

VARIATIONS OF COUPLES THERAPY

"If you come to a fork in the road, take it."

—Yogi Berra

THIS BOOK WOULDN'T be complete without an overview of the variety of formats in which couples therapy can occur. These include premarital couples therapy, discernment counseling, marathon couples therapy, group couples therapy, and sex therapy.

PREMARITAL COUPLES THERAPY

If you get married in the United States, there's roughly a 50 percent chance that your marriage will end in divorce, even though most wedding vows proclaim you'll stay together "till death do you part."[50] There's a strong statistical chance—equal to the flip of a coin—that at some point, you could run into fatal problems with the relationship you're in now.

Increasingly, new couples are turning to premarital counseling to stave off what some have called an epidemic of failed marriages and committed relationships. There's strong evidence suggesting that investing in some form of relationship therapy during the early stage of your relationship gives you a better-than-average chance of beating the odds of your relationship failing. Some research has indicated that if you learn the basic relationship skills that are commonly taught in many premarital counseling or premarital education programs, you may cut your risk of divorce by 30 percent.[51]

Research is consistently clear about the physical and mental health benefits of being in a lasting, committed relationship. Studies that have followed couples for twenty years or more indicate that if you have a satisfying relationship, you'll live longer, suffer fewer health problems, and even sustain fewer accidents.[52] The quality of your relationship matters also, of course. The more conflict in your relationship, the greater the risk you have of experiencing medical and mental health issues. Last but not least, there's strong evidence that children raised within environments that are based on intact and stable marriages are more able to thrive physically and emotionally.

There are effective resources available to help couples

---

50   http://www.cdc.gov/nchs/mardiv.htm

51   www.ncbi.nlm.nih.gov/pubmed/16569096

52   http://onlinelibrary.wiley.com/doi/10.1111/jomf.12025/full

strengthen their marriage and prevent its collapse. Yet many couples either don't know about these resources or don't take advantage of them fully. In my experience, couples miss out on the benefits of premarital counseling for reasons that stem from three central myths:

THREE MYTHS ABOUT PREMARITAL COUNSELING

It's just for couples having trouble with their relationship.

Seeing a couples therapist when things are going well will make the relationship worse.

The engagement program required for many church weddings is the same as premarital counseling with a couples therapist.

FACT: Going to premarital counseling doesn't mean that you're having trouble with your relationship.

Many couples seek premarital counseling when the waters are calm. Waiting too long to learn fundamental relationship skills is perhaps the number-one killer of relationships. Finding a premarital counselor or relationship enhancement course at the start of your relationship—when trust, cooperation, and respect are usually highest—can establish healthy habits and help you avoid serious difficulties later.

It's also definitely true that couples with relatively serious concerns are common premarital counseling seekers. If you're struggling with how to align your lives as a new couple (this pertains especially to older couples or divorcees), or wonder if you're making the right choice (cold feet), premarital counseling is a highly effective way to gain the reassurance and skills you need to prevent divorce.

FACT: Talking to a couples therapist when you don't have major concerns doesn't mean that you'll make things worse.

I hear a lot of people, especially men, start premarital counseling with me by saying, "I'm doing this for her." Basically the guy says, "I think we're fine, but she's got concerns I want you to help her with." Then he'll add, looking at me sideways, "Let's just not rock the boat too much, you know what I mean?"

If you're working with a trained and qualified couples therapist, you don't need to worry about therapy making your relationship more complicated. But avoid making the mistake of assuming that since you don't have major relationship problems, it will be okay to get couples counseling from any psychotherapist. Couples therapy is a specialized form of therapy and most graduate counseling programs offer little, if any, instruction in couples therapy. I hear lots of unfortunate stories from couples about their wrangles with undertrained couples therapists who claimed to have experience working with couples but were really just trying to avoid turning away business. Take the time to research your selection of a premarital therapist carefully.

FACT: Many educational programs for engaged or

pre-engaged couples have tremendous value, but are substantially different from private premarital counseling.

One of the bright facts about marriage in the United States in the last ten years is that marriage and relationship educational programs are growing quickly, as a visit to places online like www.HealthyMarriageInfo.org or www.SmartMarriages.com will confirm.[53] You can usually find a marriage and relationship course being taught near you. These courses are typically very low-cost or free, and many are taught "out-of-the-box," meaning they use a curriculum already developed by relationship experts.[54] If you can't find a course, try reaching out to local churches, which often sponsor marriage enrichment programs. It's beneficial to learn relationship skills anywhere, even in a small group, but remember that nothing quite compares to the level of attention you receive in private premarital counseling.

Private premarital counseling is usually short-term (four to twelve sessions), but it can often last for as many sessions as are needed, and it sometimes looks no different from normal couples therapy. Many clergy members offer premarital counseling, but be sure to ask how in-depth your pastor will go during the sessions. Many clergy use an educational or advice-giving format based on exploring the main topics of faith, dating history, marriage expectations, partner roles, and views

---

53   www.HealthyMarriageInfo.org and www.SmartMarriages.com are both nonprofit organizations.

54   For example, I contributed to the development of an out-of-the-box course for couples called *Couplehood as a Spiritual Path*, by Harville Hendrix.

about money, sex, and parenting. Some clergy and couples therapists alike utilize surveys and tests to assess your compatibility and highlight areas where you're alike or different. The most popular of these premarital assessment instruments is the Prepare/Enrich questionnaire.[55]

DISCERNMENT COUNSELING: TESTING THE WATERS

Few couples therapists are ever trained to effectively work with what is called the "mixed-agenda" couple, where one person wants to save the relationship and the other wants to end it. But a new form of counseling, called discernment counseling, is designed specifically with the mixed-agenda couple in mind. According to discernment counseling creator William Doherty, PhD, a researcher and couples therapy instructor at the University of Minnesota, at least 30 percent of couples coming to therapy could be categorized as mixed-agenda. Doherty started what's called the Minnesota Couples on the Brink Project as a way to provide leadership in the field of marriage therapy for this often-ignored segment of couples.[56]

According to Doherty, mixed-agenda couples need couples therapists to throw out their standard "bag of tricks." Too often, couples therapists treat mixed-agenda couples as "those who can't be helped." Fortunately, the Couples on the Brink Project began labeling this problem, raising awareness among

---

55 www.prepare-enrich.com

56 www.discernmentcounseling.com

therapists and training them with specific interventions that are effective for mixed-agenda couples.

Discernment counseling is distinct from standard couples counseling in these ways:

- It's short-term counseling (a maximum of five counseling sessions).

- The focus is not on solving relationship problems, but on seeing if they can *potentially* be solved.

- Unlike traditional couples therapy, which assumes that both people are willing to work on the relationship, discernment counseling helps couples decide whether to attempt to repair the relationship, to end it, or to decide what to do later.

- Sessions are split between individual time and couple time.

- The discernment counselor works to build trust with each partner, helping the leaning-out person make a decision about whether to work on the relationship, and helping the leaning-in person bring his or her best self to the crisis in hopes that the marriage can be salvaged and improved. The goal is to become clear about whether to work on the relationship or not. When a decision emerges, the counselor either commences with couples therapy based on a reconciliation plan, or helps the parties find other professionals such as mediators or collaborative divorce lawyers who can help them have a constructive divorce if that's the direction they choose.

Discernment counselors can also be helpful for one person even if your partner doesn't want to participate. However, according to the Couples on the Brink website, discernment counseling is not appropriate in the following instances:

- One spouse has made a final decision to divorce and wants counseling to encourage the other spouse to accept that decision.

- There's a danger of domestic violence.

- There's an Order of Protection from the court.

- One partner is coercing the other to participate.

The Couples on the Brink project actively certifies couples therapists as discernment counselors in the United States.[57]

You may also find many experienced couples and family counselors who practice some version of Doherty's discernment counseling, but they don't name it as such or advertise it specifically. Use what you've learned about the concept of discernment counseling to have a conversation with the therapist you're considering to find out how well he or she can implement this newer and highly useful precursor to couples therapy.

---

57   An up-to-date directory of discernment counselors can be found at: www.DiscernmentCounseling.com

MARATHON COUPLES THERAPY

Marathon couples therapy is a unique form of intensive therapy that deserves special mention. In marathon sessions, you and your partner meet privately with one therapist for a short but continuous period of time, usually over the course of successive days. This rare option isn't recommended for all couples, since even weekly sessions are intensive enough for most people. But for couples facing an impending deadline, like an overseas military deployment or a wedding date, marathon couples therapy can be very useful. The format of marathon couples therapy may include completion of an entire couples therapy educational workbook, sometimes under the personal direction of the author of that material. Because it provides personal attention for an extended and continuous duration, marathon couples counseling can have a big impact if you and your partner are stuck in a difficult pattern.

GROUP COUPLES THERAPY

Couples therapy groups are not as popular as they used to be. At the peak of the popularity of group therapy, in the 1960s and 1970s, you could find many couples therapists who offered different types of groups from which you could choose. For example, you might have found a couples therapy group specifically composed of couples recovering from infidelity, couples that were new parents, or couples that wanted to improve communication. Today, you may be lucky to find one or two couples therapy groups in your area that meet regularly or that are open to new members. If you do find a couples therapy group, expect that it will be limited to ten members or fewer, will be closed to new members once the group starts, and may either meet for an indefinite period of time or have a specific start and end date.

One of the reasons for the decline of group couples therapy is the level of intensity they create, compared with private therapy or educational courses. While many therapists argue that the personal relationships that are forged in therapy groups are what makes them so powerful and able to challenge "stuck" behaviors, not everyone feels comfortable sharing personal details with others. If you want to get a behind-the-scenes look at an in-depth couples therapy group, pick up a copy of the book Laurie Abraham wrote about the year she spent embedded in one as a journalist. *The Husbands and Wives Club: A Year in the Life of a Couples Therapy Group* gives you a play-by-play account of what group couples counseling looks like with an experienced and eclectic therapist who used both attachment and behavioral methods.

SEX THERAPY

All couples are bound to have differences of opinion about bedroom behavior. But don't make the mistake of assuming that the average couples counselor is competent to help you address specific sexual issues. Sex therapy is a specialized form of psychotherapy that focuses on specific sexual concerns. A sex therapist is someone who is able to treat sexual dysfunction that can include:

- Lack of sex between partners.

- Low desire for sex.

- Inability to reach or difficulty in reaching orgasm.

- Performance concerns (difficulty with erection or premature ejaculation).

- Pain during intercourse (dyspareunia).

- Difficulty communicating about sex.

- Healing from sexual abuse or trauma.

- Sexual arousal dysfunctions.

- Sexual addiction.

- Sexual identity issues.

- Exploration of sexual preferences.

Sex therapists are licensed psychotherapists who receive special post-graduate education and training to treat sexual issues with both couples and individuals. The American Association of Sexuality Educators, Counselors and Therapists (AASECT) provides rigorous certification and ethics standards for sex therapists and sex educators, and maintains a directory of certified professionals.[58] Because sex therapists are in high demand, few participate in health insurance networks. This doesn't mean you can't find a sex therapist who takes your insurance, or who has

---

58   www.aasect.org

a reduced fee. But you may have to carefully interview several to assess the quality of prospective in-network therapists and to learn more about their backgrounds (see Chapter 7).

Since the topic of sexual issues is very important to couples, I feel it's important to include extra discussion about the important sex therapy resources available.

CAN WE GET HELP FOR SEXUAL ISSUES FROM OUR COUPLES THERAPIST?

Although you might expect any couples therapist would be able to help you with sexual intimacy issues, this is not necessarily true. Similarly, not all sex therapists are good at providing general couples therapy, and may not be aware of the sophisticated attachment-based couples therapies highlighted in the first two parts of this book. As when choosing any therapist, if you want to address sexual intimacy in couples therapy, carefully interview any prospective therapist. Some sex therapists may practice behavioral or solution-focused therapy, not attachment-based therapy. This means sexual issues could be treated principally with exercises designed to help you either create new habits or extinguish unhelpful habits. If focusing on the emotional issues involved in your sexual intimacy— not just focusing on exercises to help you change your behavior—is important to you, consider searching for a sex therapist who's also familiar with attachment-based couples therapy. A sex therapist who's also trained in one of the Big Three couples therapies described in this book could potentially integrate both behavioral and emotional or attachment-based techniques.

Deborah Fox, a sex therapist based in Washington, DC, who is also trained in Imago couples therapy, teaches other couples therapists that they can treat many common intimacy issues with good couples counseling if they have some basic knowledge about sexual dysfunction and a high comfort level with discussing explicit topics.

"Not everyone who wants a better sex life needs a sex therapist," says Fox. "But especially if you're dealing with recovery from sexual trauma, sexual addiction, or symptoms of sexual dysfunction in addition to standard [individual] treatment for the trauma or addiction, these are also things you're going to need the expertise of a sex therapist for. If you find a great couples therapist who is also a sex therapist, that's definitely a win-win."

FOUR IMPORTANT QUESTIONS MOST COUPLES DON'T ASK ABOUT SEX THERAPY

You're definitely not alone if talking about sex makes you uncomfortable. However, for the best outcome in your therapy experience, it's critical that you speak candidly to any prospective therapist you interview about their experiences with helping couples improve sexual intimacy.

The basic question to ask is: "How would you help us with _____ issue?" In addition, here are four specific questions that many couples may not think to ask a prospective sex therapist:

- *How do you work with a couple that is uncertain about whether they need mainly couples therapy or sex therapy?*

This question can be helpful in assessing if your therapist primarily sees herself as a sex therapist, a couples therapist, or a hybrid of both. For example, does she treat a man's concern that he is not equally matched to his wife's lower sex drive by using a strictly "try-this and try-that," approach? If the therapist sticks to solution-focused methods only, she might give his wife instructions to read erotic books and masturbate more often to naturally boost her testosterone levels and increase her sex drive. Or does the therapist use her training as a couples therapist to help him (or her, if the situation is reversed) address the libido difference in the relationship by creating attachment-friendly, safer communication habits that lead to greater acceptance of their differences? Or does the therapist use some combination of both solution-focused advice and attention to emotional issues involved?

- *What kind of cultural and subcultural biases do you have that might inform how you advise people to handle sexual concerns?*

Some sex therapists consider themselves *sexologists*, therapists highly educated in the scientific and academic aspects of sexual function. Others have received some education about sex therapy but draw primarily on a wide range of their own personal and clinical experiences with sex. Many couples wander into their first sex therapy session completely unaware of whether their therapist will be compatible with their own cultural or religious values regarding sex. Be sure to clearly state what your values are and ask your prospective therapist to share his or hers. Do you prefer to work with someone who has more of an "anything goes" attitude toward sex, or someone with more conservative views who has expertise with sexual issues?

• *How do you help couples with sexual issues that have caused harm to their core relationship?*

If you're finding that The Four Horsemen of the Apocalypse (Contempt, Stonewalling, Resentment, and Criticism [see Chapter 5]) are galloping into your relationship and your therapist ignores them to spend four weeks focusing instead on sexual performance concerns about your husband, it should raise a red flag. Try to find out how well your therapist knows the attachment-based methods described in Part I. How does she integrate the behavioral aspects of sex therapy (using exercises designed to increase desired behaviors and decrease undesired behaviors) with the "softer" and more complex goals of creating safety and emotional connection to your partner?

• *Are there any sexual issues that you don't feel qualified to address or comfortable addressing?*

Generally speaking, sex therapists are especially accepting people. It's not easy to make a sex therapist blush or become uncomfortable with something you're dealing with. But remember, you're shopping for a "human product," and making an assumption about the biases of your sex therapist may be a sure way to end up having a negative therapy experience. The best approach is to be candid about the issue you want help with—before you start treatment—and ask how (and how frequently) the therapist works with your issue. Even the language your therapist uses to explain how he'll help your situation will tell you a lot. Does he use the same words you're comfortable using to refer to body parts, or is he using slang that doesn't feel appropriate to you? These are small, but important cues to pay attention to. If you don't feel confident that he or she is comfortable with your specific issue, don't be afraid to ask for a referral.

HOW SEX THERAPY WORKS

First of all, let's put to bed the myth that sex therapy involves any sort of physical contact between you and your therapist or that you and your partner would have physical contact during sessions with your therapist. All sessions with reputable sex therapists are strictly talk therapy.[59] However, no topic of

---

59   In recent years, a highly controversial, (and very rare) practice called sexual surrogacy has sprouted in the U.S. and abroad. A sexual surrogate is paid to provide a type of physical and talk therapy that *includes* sexual contact and is designed to help individuals overcome severe sexual phobias, traumas, or the inability to maintain a sexual partner. In the 2012 movie *The Sessions,* Helen Hunt plays a sexual surrogate who works with a man attached to an iron lung machine. Although the profession is regulated by the International

conversation is taboo with a sex therapist. Sex therapists are comfortable with talking matter-of-factly about any aspect of sex, and part of their job is to educate clients about sexual physiology and anatomy. On the one hand, they can diagnose and treat sexual dysfunctions like hypoarousal disorders (low sex drive), sexless relationships (defined as sex less than twice per month), or dyspareunia (painful intercourse). They can help you overcome low self-esteem and improve your body image—the feelings you have about the way you look and feel physically. A sex therapist can also help you spice up life in the bedroom even if you don't have a serious problem. It's normal for couples to get into a rut doing the same things in the bedroom they've done for years. Sometimes it's helpful to have a unbiased third party offer suggestions and challenge old habits in a way that's comfortable and respectful for both of you.

Depending on the issues you want to address, sex therapy can be anywhere between a relatively brief "drive-through" done in four sessions, or it may involve a prolonged treatment plan that progresses over the course of a year. Most commonly, sex therapy sessions are attended by both you and your partner. However, if your partner won't go to therapy with you or you have a strong preference to not invite your partner, individual sex therapy can still be very beneficial to you.

Usually a sex therapist will interview you and your partner together and then separately during the first one to three sessions. Next, the therapist will present an assessment and

Professional Surrogates Association and has a code of ethics, all counseling professions consider sexual contact of any kind between a therapist and client to be unethical and grounds for the revocation of a state license.

propose a treatment plan. Once you and your partner receive an assessment, it will usually be clear whether there are any sexual issues that require additional treatment resources. Not every sex therapist, for example, offers the specialized care needed to treat symptoms of female pain during intercourse or the inability to climax. These are issues that even many gynecologists are not adequately trained to address in a sensitive and effective manner. For some kinds of sexual pain, a qualified sex therapist may work with a roster of trusted gynecologists and physical therapists.

Once you and your therapist have agreed upon the areas you want to address, your sessions will focus on the specific mechanics of the issue, and you'll often be assigned "homework" assignments. These are suggestions you can test in real life, with or sometimes without your partner, then come back to the next session with feedback. You make adjustments to the exercises and try again, or you progress to more challenging exercises.

One common exercise given to many couples in sex therapy is called *sensate focusing*. "Often couples have either gotten into ruts with their sexual routines, or have so little time that they rush through foreplay, and don't take the necessary time to get fully aroused," says Lauren Jordan, a sex therapist in Dallas. To mentally break the connection between sex and the pressure to perform, sex is decreed off-limits during or after sensate focusing. The exercise instructs couples to reconnect with non-genital touch, going slow enough to figure out what feels pleasurable.

In summary, sex therapy is a highly specialized form of

talk therapy that many couples undertake as an alternative or adjunct to regular couples therapy. Some couples therapists are very skilled at addressing basic concerns about sexual intimacy, while others may be unprepared or uncomfortable with the subject. Similarly, while most sex therapists are skilled at couples therapy and will help you with other areas of your relationship, some sex therapists have limited expertise in the intricacies of couples therapy. Be prepared to interview a prospective sex therapist before you start sessions, to ensure that you and your partner feel comfortable with his or her style and approach to addressing your specific concerns.

CHAPTER 9

ALTERNATIVES TO COUPLES THERAPY

"If you want something in life you've never had,
you'll have to do something you've never done."

—J.D. Houston

F OR MANY COUPLES, there's no substitute for the dedicated attention of a qualified couples therapist. For others, an intensive weekend retreat, relationship coach, self-help educational product, or online program can be very effective. You may want to consider such alternatives to couples therapy, or some combination of both, if your situation fits one of the following scenarios:

- You're preparing for marriage or have no serious concerns about your relationship, but want to stay on a good course together.

- Your experiences with couples therapy were so difficult that you aren't ready to start the process again.

- You can't afford to pay for couples therapy.

- You want to enhance your couples therapy with complementary educational experiences.

There are vast resources available that are excellent alternatives to one-on-one couples counseling. This chapter will give you an overview of these options.

WEEKEND INTENSIVES FOR COUPLES

Each of the Big Three leading brands of couples counseling highlighted in this book has developed educational workshops that you can attend independent of participating in couples therapy. These workshops are held in most states and in many countries around the world. In addition to limited public events held by the authors of the curriculum, these workshops are usually taught by people who have been certified to teach the course by that brand's parent organization. Many of those certified to present these workshops are also couples therapists, but some, while trained to lead the workshops, are not formally trained in therapy.

Each of these workshops combines lectures, video presentations, live demonstrations, and private time for you to complete personal exercises or have conversations with your partner. Public sharing is usually limited to those who volunteer to demonstrate a particular exercise.

Some people find tremendous benefit from attending a workshop, perhaps in combination with reading one or more of the recommended books associated with a particular brand of therapy (these books are listed at the end of Chapters 4, 5, and 6). One of the reasons I labeled the therapies mentioned in this book the Big Three is because they each have published several popular, extremely readable books that are written for a general audience.

I've often received positive feedback from couples who attend an educational workshop in conjunction with couples therapy. They find that the combination of learning through lecture and observation and learning experientially in couples therapy is quite helpful. One couple told me they had a major breakthrough during a weekend Imago workshop and, as a result, more clearly understood some of the features of their sessions in private couples therapy. Before attending the Imago workshop, the husband bristled at the concept of intentional dialogue. But after seeing how the dialogue exercise helped calm down an overreactive spouse during the couples workshop, he bought into the idea. "To be honest," the husband later told me, "I was getting frustrated [in our sessions] and I was ready to quit. But now I get it. It's brilliant, actually. Now I'm ready to buckle down and do the work in therapy."

You don't have to participate in couples therapy to get benefits from weekend intensives. And you don't have to attend one of the Big Three weekend workshops to really help your relationship. For a list of some of the weekend intensives available for couples, go to: www.MarriageHelpAdvisor.com.

RELATIONSHIP COACHES

Some couples find that working with a professional coach is a viable alternative to couples therapy; some find that working only with a coach is inadequate for their situation. Others choose to work with both a coach and a therapist. Coaching in the United States is not regulated by state boards of health as psychotherapy is, and it therefore has a reputation for being a less formal method of getting help for your relationship. A coach is like a personal consultant who assumes you and your partner are generally healthy and capable of making changes if given guidance and information. Coaches tend to focus exclusively on achieving goals and are likely to steer you away from discussing emotional issues in your past. Coaches specialize in just about any area of concern that you might have. In addition to relationship coaching, other types of coaching fall under the catchall phrase of "life coach." There are business coaches, dating coaches, divorce coaches, executive coaches, financial coaches, grief coaches, parenting coaches, and spiritual coaches.

Coaching became especially popular in the 1990s, when therapists started leaving health insurance networks and needed new ways to market their services. Many psychotherapists also market themselves as coaches because of the increasing appetite for quick solutions and answers to problems among couples seeking help. One of the leading coaching organizations, International Coach Foundation (ICF), has more than 20,000 members.[60] By ICF's estimates, 40 percent of its members are also psychotherapists, and one in five therapists are coaches.

---

60   www.CoachFederation.org

Some of the attractions of relationship coaching are: it tends to be advice-oriented; it can be done over the phone; meetings can be brief (thirty-minute sessions are common); and it can be done on an as-needed basis. Coaches may draw on many of the same psychological theories as therapists, including attachment theory. However, most coaches tend to emphasize positive psychology—an approach that focuses on finding strengths and solutions (rather than identifying problems), and on living to your fullest potential. Going to a relationship coach isn't recommended if you're having serious relationship upheaval accompanied by emotional distress or symptoms of a mental health disorder. As one life coach website states, "If therapists are surgeons, coaches are personal trainers."

Here's one example of a couple who benefited from a relationship coach. Chris and James called a coach when they hit a rough patch. James had been laid off from his job and started spending a lot more time around the house, which led to more tension in the relationship than either one of them were comfortable with. "We wanted to make some improvements, but it just felt easier to say, 'we're talking to a coach' compared to 'we're in therapy,'" said James. "We still felt we had a lot of kick in our relationship but wanted more."

In many ways, Chris and James were the perfect candidates for relationship coaching. Their relationship was stable and little damage had been done by their recent struggles adapting to James's unemployment. They both had experience receiving individual psychotherapy and were certain and articulate about the potential issues that were currently causing them problems. Although many couples in their situation would benefit equally from either working with a couples therapist or a relationship coach, Chris and James wanted to reserve the option of couples therapy for any relationship problems that they couldn't make sense of themselves. At that point, they preferred the light touch of relationship coaching, but remained open to more intensive couples therapy if their coach suggested it later.

Although there are some clear distinctions between relationship coaching and couples therapy, the line between the two can be quite blurry. For example, many therapists will tell you they're trained to do everything that a coach does and more. So is coaching simply a repackaged "therapy lite" marketing strategy for mental health professionals? Not necessarily. It's important to know that, depending on the type of therapy and the style of the therapist to which you compare coaching, the differences can be vast or relatively small.

HOW RELATIONSHIP COACHING COMPARES TO RELATIONSHIP THERAPY

Relationship coaching and relationship therapy have several similarities and differences. It's important to know how the two compare before you make a decision about whom to ask for help. Keep in mind that—like couples therapy—the quality of services you receive depends a lot on the individual coach you hire.

Relationship Coaching	Relationship Therapy
Clients are fully capable of reaching goals.	Clients need help removing obstacles that stop them from reaching goals.
Philosophy: Focus is on known goals and taking action.	Philosophy: Goals and taking action are a part of overall purpose of personal/emotional growth and healing.
Takes place commonly by phone, online, or in person.	In person only, with rare exceptions over the phone or online.
You can expect: Candid reactions, humorous coach-speak: "How are you going to make this happen?" Coach gives straight-forward instructions and holds clients accountable.	You can expect: Composure, more filtered reactions. You can expect: Therapist will often ask you to tap into emotions with questions like, "How does that make you feel?" May use pointed inter-pretations: "It seems like you're avoiding your wife in the same the way you learned to distance yourself from your mother."
Contact between sessions expected.	Limited contact between sessions (for crises only).

Relationship Coaching	Relationship Therapy
Not state licensed. No training requirements needed to advertise as a coach.	State license required. Graduate degree plus 1,500-3,000 supervised client contact hours required before therapist can receive independent license.
Will not focus on childhood or offer emotional development strategies.	Often focuses on childhood or emotional development, depending on goals of therapy.
Cost per hour range: $60-$300	Cost per hour range: $100-$300

Many relationship coaches—like couples therapists—specialize in specific areas. In general, coaches seem comfortable aggressively marketing themselves, and they aren't as afraid to put personal information about themselves in their blog, Twitter feed, or on their professional Facebook page. But according to Dina Zeckhausen, a therapist who's been practicing in Atlanta for twenty years, many therapists have begun to adapt to clients' expectations of a more personal connection with a therapist. "It used to be that if somebody asked about the therapist's personal life, he or she would reflect that back and interpret why the person is asking the question and what it means," she said. "People don't put up with that anymore. If you're that way, they'll say: 'That therapist was so aloof. I felt so uncomfortable. It was such a weird interaction.'"[61]

Because coaching is unregulated by state health licensing boards, you need to choose a coach wisely. Relationship coaches usually begin their clinical practice after achieving a certification by one of several life coach training institutions. But according to Dr. Dawn-Elise Snipes—an expert witness for legal cases involving life coaches—because anyone can hang a shingle to offer advice as a coach, there's no legal accountability for services provided by a coach.[62] If you're interested in pursuing relationship or life coaching, I suggest that you apply the same principles discussed in this book for finding guidance from a couples therapist: find a coach who understands the latest and most complex ideas about couples, such as attachment theory, and trust your own ideas about what you need from him or her to help you build a trusting professional partnership.

Further Reading on Coaching

Jim Paterson, "Counseling vs. Life Coaching," *Counseling Today*, www.ct.counseling.org

Geoff Williams, *Divorce Coach: 3 Things A Divorce Coach Can Do For You.* www.huffingtonpost.com

---

61   Lori Gottlieb, "What Brand Is Your Therapist?" New York Times Magazine, November 23, 2012, www.nytimes.com.

62   Life Coaching: "An End Run Around Counseling Practice Acts," accessed April 16, 2014, www.hgexperts.com

Lynn Grodzki, "The Coaching Edge: Helping Clients Take Their Best Shot," *Psychotherapy Networker*, www.psychotherapynetworker.org.

RELATIONSHIP SELF-HELP: THE (SOMETIMES) UNHAPPY MARRIAGE OF PROFESSIONAL HELP AND SELF-HELP

"We should be giving our knowledge away so that it can really be of use to people in improving their lives. We shouldn't be hoarding what we know to protect our economic self-interests."

—George Albee, former president of the American Psychological Association

I believe that most self-help, educational resources, and couples workshops can be beneficial to couples—and they don't have to be mutually exclusive with professional therapy. But if you run a quick online search for relationship self-help, you'll find many self-help gurus who seem to paint professional counseling in a negative light. From a marketing perspective, it makes sense to differentiate yourself from the competition as much as possible. But in my opinion, some online programs go too far and seem to denigrate traditional therapy. Some programs also make claims about the outcome of buying their product, which professional counselors are barred from doing by ethical standards. As long as we live in a world where people have to make a living, there will always be a dichotomy between self-help and professional help. Some educational and self-help resources are quite compatible with couples counseling, and many couples have commented that they get more value from couples counseling by investing the time to participate in a particular self-help curriculum, and vice versa.

I've put together a special section on my website, www. MarriageHelpAdvisor.com, that highlights a few of what I consider the best of these self-help programs. In the interest of full disclosure: I've taken time to become personally familiar with some of these programs and may have an affiliate relationship with some of them. This means that as a business partner, I might receive a small financial compensation from them if you use one of their programs. The Internet is chock full of advice cleverly packaged to appeal to any crisis you might have in your relationship. I've carefully vetted a few of these online resources to help you avoid indiscriminately choosing a self-study program to help you and your relationship.

ONLINE SELF-HELP FOR RELATIONSHIPS: HOW TO PROCEED WISELY

When you turn to the web for advice about your relationship, know that your search results may vary. Actually, this is an understatement. The Internet has the potential to link us with many wonderful and bright ideas that could enhance who we are. At the same time, be wary of being exposed to many strange ideas online that can be confusing or harmful. To help sort through the jungle of information about relationships online, here are a few of the more reputable sites that I have vetted and have seen actually help people:

www.SmartMarriages.com

This is an online clearinghouse for all things related to educational programs for couples (not just about marriage). This website is a carefully curated collection of books, live and online courses, and events that support healthy relationships.

www.TalkAboutMarriage.com

This is for those of you willing to post personal experiences online. It's a relationship forum, and is one of the most highly trafficked destinations for people seeking relationship advice from peers. It contains frank—and not always balanced—discussions on relationship topics (not just marriage) ranging from infidelity to sex, communication, dating, separation, and divorce. The Talk About Marriage (TAM) forum even has a section for reviews of online self-help materials, and one thread devoted to sharing therapy experiences. The conversations are lively and sometimes intense, and unfriendly contributors (in online parlance, "trolls") are moderated by a dedicated group of volunteers. Anyone can easily search the hundreds of thousands of threads—the online term for a chain of messages related to a single topic—on every imaginable topic involving a relationship, but to post a comment you must create an online *avatar,* or online identity.

Most avatars on the TAM forum are anonymous pseudonyms.

However, what makes this site particularly useful is that trained couples counselors also participate on the forum and its sister site, www.Family-Marriage-Counseling.com, which is a state-by-state directory of relationship counselors. Like most online forums, posts on TAM are visible to nonmembers. That means your post is visible to anyone searching the web. When participating in any online forum, it's important to carefully read that website's privacy policy and follow its rules about etiquette on the forum. For example, posting information on TAM that identifies another person's real identity without their permission is not allowed. Such posts are quickly flagged as inappropriate and removed, and subject the author to being banned from the site. On TAM your personal information, including your email address, is hidden by default unless you choose to make it public.

CHAPTER 10

THE SEARCH FOR THE RIGHT THERAPIST

"The way to find a needle in a haystack is to sit down."

—Beryl Markham, *West with the Night*

I N MARCH 2012, the *New York Times* published an article entitled "Does Couples Therapy Work?" It highlighted some of the potential pitfalls of couples therapy, but chiefly the fact that many therapists perform couples therapy without having received any specialized training. A 2011 edition of one of the psychotherapy field's most popular magazines, *Psychotherapy Networker*, also trumpeted the fact that people could end up with a couples therapist who's more afraid of couples therapy than you are! One article pointed out that while few graduate counseling programs teach courses in couples therapy, most therapists offer this service. If you're considering throwing yourself into the ring with a couples therapist anytime soon, this should be eye opening. But don't panic.

In Parts I and II, you learned the basics of attachment theory. This knowledge should help you and your partner recognize and be comfortable with the major concepts behind many therapies. Perhaps you even feel ready to make an informed decision about what kind of couples therapist you'd prefer to work with. Maybe attachment-based therapy resonates with you. Perhaps it doesn't. You may have decided that attachment-based therapy isn't for you. Or, like most people, you'll opt for a therapist who integrates several different types of therapy; perhaps he or she will mix one of the attachment-based therapies *and* a solution-focused behavioral method. The most important thing is this: spend time becoming familiar with what goes on inside some of the leading couples therapies today, so that you may develop an informed opinion about what you need. *This is one of the most critical factors in determining the success of your therapy.*

WORKING WITH AN UNLICENSED THERAPIST RESIDENT OR INTERN

You may run into some counselors practicing while still residents or interns. This simply means that his or her work will be supervised by a licensed counselor while the hours needed for license certification are being met. The benefit of working with an unlicensed, supervised therapist is that the cost of your sessions should be considerably less than a licensed therapist would charge. The obvious drawback is lack of experience. However, I've known resident couples counselors who are quite proficient and attuned to the complexities of relationship therapy. Choosing an unlicensed counselor who intends to specialize in couples therapy may be a better decision than choosing a licensed counselor with another focus.

If cost is a factor but you'd like a check-and-balance system in place before signing on with a less experienced couples counselor, consider working with a therapist being supervised by a senior counselor—perhaps someone who trains or supervises other therapists in Imago Relationship Therapy, Emotion-Focused Couples Therapy, or the Gottman Method Couples Counseling. Certification is a rigorous process. Ask a supervisor to recommend an unlicensed couples therapist under his or her supervision. Despite the relative inexperience of an intern or resident, having supervision means you'll essentially be receiving two therapists for the price of one. I personally think this can be the best of both worlds—it just takes some research on your part to find the "diamonds in the rough." There will be gifted therapists out there who haven't yet accumulated the contact hours needed for licensure.

THE FIRST CRITERION: VALID LICENSURE

In order to provide the service of "therapy, counseling, psychotherapy, or marriage counseling," a practitioner must be licensed by the state in which he or she practices. This means the counselor has earned at least a master's degree within their mental health discipline, has passed a licensing exam, and has accumulated supervised client-contact hours ranging from 1,500 to 3,000 total.

A valid license indicates an important legal and ethical standing. It means that the counselor is accountable to a state health licensing board for actions conducted during therapy. A licensed counselor also must maintain a clean criminal record and attend yearly continuing education courses, some of which must focus on ethical practices. A license can't tell you, though, whether a therapist is competent or if he or she has the training and experience necessary to help you. A series of sample interview questions at the end of this chapter are designed to help you screen a potential therapist, to help you assess his or her competence in couples therapy, and to help you decide if a therapist's approach to couples counseling is right for you and your partner.

You can—and should—check to see if the therapist you're considering is in good ethical and legal standing with his or her profession's board of health. A useful web resource, www.checkatherapist.com, has links to all state health boards so you can search for any practitioner's license verification.

WHERE DO I SEARCH FOR A THERAPIST?

The first place many people turn to when trying to find a therapist is to provider listings issued by their health insurance company. Before you assume this is the best way to proceed, however, stop to consider the pros and cons of using your health insurance. That topic is discussed in detail in Chapter

7. Below are other common methods of finding a therapist. You may also want to consult with one of the many professional associations for counselors that provide a searchable therapist directory (see Appendix B).

Word of Mouth

The oldest way to find a therapist is to simply ask friends, clergy, or your doctor for a good referral. Technology has expanded on our ability to tap into these types of social networks, and specialty websites now provide ratings of doctors or service providers. You might not want to publically broadcast the fact that you're having relationship issues on your neighborhood online message board right along with requests for plumbers. But doing so tactfully will likely yield a lot of responses and recommendations from people who might also be willing to share some of their personal experiences.

Phone Books and Yellow Pages

Believe it or not, you'll still find names of therapists in a phone book or the Yellow Pages. That's great if you've amassed a list of names and just need to contact one of them, but cold-calling practitioners is of course not an effective way to search for something as important as a couples counselor. Generally speaking, therapists who get the majority of their new business from phone book results fall into two categories: they either have a successful practice already and don't need any more business (perhaps from having been in business a long time), or they don't have many clients because they aren't using technology effectively to reach the majority of people searching for their services. The point is that online channels of communication are far more sophisticated and yield better results.

Online Search Results

Go to your favorite Internet search engine (Google, Bing, Yahoo, etc.), and simply type in "couples therapist [name of your town]." For example: "couples therapist Springfield Missouri," and you'll get dozens of pages of results. Keep in mind that there are two kinds of search results you get: *paid ads* and *organic search results*.

Paid ads on Google are designed to deceptively blend in with organic results, but are usually the first three or four results at the top or side of your screen. Organic search results show you websites that most closely match your search query. The top-ranked organic search results are usually the sites most relevant to your search phrase, as well as those most heavily trafficked online by others looking for what you are. It's easy for a therapist to pay so that his or her business appears at the top of search result ads whenever certain words are typed in. If a therapist appears on the first few pages of the organic search results, however, it's for a reason. The latter usually have a high "reputation" in the eyes of Google.

When you're searching for a therapist online, I recommend adding descriptive words to your search terms, then comparing both the organic and paid results. For example, "couples therapist Springfield" will give you more specific results than just "couples therapist," and "infidelity couples therapist springfield" will give you even better results, if you want help with sorting out an affair.

Most therapists have at least a simple website now. Take advantage of how the competition to find clients has compelled therapists to present their practices in great detail online. Browsing a therapist's website will reveal a lot about the specific kind of couples counseling being offered, and sometimes they'll have links to videos or audio presentations as well.

Online Therapist Directories

When you type in a search term related to "counseling" or "psychotherapy," many of the first-page results will be online therapist directories. These directories conveniently pool together the profiles of dozens or hundreds of therapists close to your geographic location. The following are some of the most comprehensive therapist directories:

- www.PsychologyToday.com

- www.Theravive.com

- www.Counsel-Search.com

- www.NetworkTherapy.com

- www.GoodTherapy.com

These sites do not recommend or endorse the therapists listed there; to be listed a therapist simply pays a monthly fee.

Specialty Online Directories

If there is one idea from this book I would want you to take away, it's to invest the time necessary to find a therapist who lives for and loves working with couples. One relatively effective shortcut to finding these therapists in a crowded online "room" is to use one of the online directories dedicated solely to couples therapy. One of them is www.Family-Marriage-Counseling.com. Another is the Registry of Marriage-Friendly Therapists: www.MarriageFriendlyTherapists.com.

THE REGISTRY OF MARRIAGE-FRIENDLY THERAPISTS

MarriageFriendlyTherapists.com is an online directory of couples therapists who have paid to distinguish themselves from others in the couples therapy field by advertising explicitly as therapists in favor of preserving relationships whenever possible.

Marriage and family therapist William Doherty founded the registry in 2005 as a way to guide couples away from therapy offered by inexperienced therapists or therapists who undermine fragile relationships because of a clinical practice that focuses too much on personal happiness instead of overcoming marriage difficulties. A leader in the field and a frequent speaker on the topic of marriage therapy, Doherty wondered how and why a majority of therapists were able to offer marriage therapy when most graduate training programs don't even require one course in relationship treatment. He states, "From a consumer's point of view, going in for couples therapy [with the average psychotherapist that isn't specially trained as a couples therapist] is like having your broken leg set by a doctor who skipped orthopedics in medical school."

As of the date of this printing, Doherty had sold www.MarriageFriendlyTherapists.com and launched a new online directory for couples therapy that he intends to be "a bolder version" of the first one with "a lot more clinical wisdom on the website through audios, e-books, articles, and more." You can find it at www.DiscernmentCounseling.com.

TEN QUESTIONS TO ASK WHEN SEARCHING FOR A COUPLES COUNSELOR

I'm always surprised when I'm talking to a prospective client but they don't have any questions for me. Consider your first conversation with a potential therapist to be an interview. Don't just share information about your own situation. Ask the therapist to share information about themselves and how or whether they've helped people in a similar situation to yours before.

1. *Tell me about your educational background. Where did you learn to provide couples therapy? Have you been the recipient of couples therapy before?*

   If the therapist is only self-taught or can't demonstrate significant education or professional certification in couples therapy that included supervision, consider going elsewhere. Most states' health licensing boards don't require therapists-in-training to receive therapy themselves, but some graduate programs do. Usually therapists who have participated in therapy themselves later say that they can't imagine providing therapy to others without having had such an important experience—this was certainly the case for me.

2. *If my partner and I aren't sure if we want to stay together, how would you guide us?*

If the therapist uses any phrases like "I try to stay neutral," or "I don't try to save marriages, I just try to help people find the best outcome," consider looking elsewhere. Relationships are critical for our health and wellbeing. A couples therapist shouldn't be leery of working to repair connections or heal hurt in a relationship, even if you and your partner don't believe it's possible when you first call. This doesn't mean all relationships are meant to continue—just be wary of therapists who seem wishy-washy about the value of working through difficulties in a committed relationship.

3. *Do you ever try to guide couples through the end of a relationship or a divorce?*

As much as attachment-based therapists are known for working to salvage difficult relationships, a reputable therapist will also know the limitations of couples therapy. He or she should be honest with you. If, after attempts to repair your attachment have repeatedly failed—which should include specific treatment recommendations for underlying causes of relationship problems such as untreated anxiety, depression, substance abuse, mental illness, or physical illness—he or she should acknowledge that sometimes the best course of action is about weighing the option to no longer be a couple.

4. *How much of your psychotherapy practice is dedicated to couples therapy?*

   Avoid therapists who mostly do individual therapy. Take the time to find a practice that can demonstrate working with a high volume or a high percentage of couples.

5. *How many couples have you treated in the last six months who are dealing with the kind of issue that I've described we are having? How do you typically help couples with this issue?*

   If the therapist says either, "Oh, too many to keep track of," or "I don't know," consider mentioning that it's important to you that you work with a therapist who doesn't just occasionally work with couples. If the number seems low or the therapist is hesitant or vague with his or her answer, ask why. You might even say, "I know a lot of therapists work mostly with individuals and think of couples therapy as basically an extension of individual therapy. I'm only interested in working with someone who focuses on couples therapy and appreciates how different it is from individual counseling."

6. *Are you yourself married or in a committed relationship now, or have you been in the past? Are you willing to*

share how your own relationship issues inform your work with couples?

Not every therapist out there will tell you his or her own track record with relationships. But in my experience, a surprising number of couples therapists are willing to be candid about their own life experiences. The answers (or nonanswers) you get can tell you a lot about how much work this person has invested in understanding himself or herself and how they have developed an approach to wrestling with common issues in relationships.

7. *How familiar are you with attachment-based couples therapy? How do you know when to help couples by using an attachment (relationship) focus and when to treat a problem that is perhaps just one partner's issue?*

Every therapist will answer this question differently. What to look for, ideally, is a therapist who understands how not to make the most common mistake made in traditional behavioral therapies: treating only the symptoms of the problem (perhaps one spouse's explosive anger) and not addressing one of the possible causes (for example, a painful loss of secure attachment in the relationship).

8. *If your therapist is trained in Imago Relationship Therapy, Emotion-Focused Therapy, or Gottman Method Couples Therapy: How much of this brand of therapy do*

you use in your sessions and when do you use it? How did you learn the method?

It can be helpful to determine how orthodox your therapist is in using a particular brand of therapy to decide whether he or she will be a good fit for you. Most therapists have heard of the popular brands of therapy—some may even advertise as offering one of those kinds of therapy, but unless you dig a little you won't know whether they passed a full certification course or merely read a book about it. Anytime someone is vague about his or her methods, be sure it's not because of inexperience. Some therapists who use these brands of therapy know how each overlaps with the other and will employ "a little bit of this and a little bit of that." Others may follow the guiding therapy's strict recipe for how to structure a session. Depending on your attitude toward each type of therapy, try to find a therapist who either uses the methods flexibly or teaches them by the book.

9. *When do you refer couples elsewhere or recommend against couples therapy?*

It's nice to know that the person you're trusting with your relationship doesn't have an unrealistic "I-can-do-everything" mentality. It's also refreshing to know if you might be considered by this therapist to be the kind of couple that he or she won't work with. For example, stepfamily couples or remarried couples tend to require an even more specialized therapeutic skill set. Other issues that should be treated by specialists are substance abuse, physical violence, sexual addiction, and mental illness. It's not uncommon for a couples therapist to recommend that individual therapy be started at the same time as couples therapy or that couples therapy only commences after a significant head-start with individual therapy for both partners.

10. *What formats can we expect our sessions with you to follow? Do you always meet with us together or sometimes separately?*

Generally, most couples therapists will tend to conduct the majority of sessions conjointly. There is no hard and fast research saying that this is better for the couple, and in some cases it's necessary for a therapist to divide sessions into private meetings to work with extreme hostility or ambivalence about the relationship (see section on Discernment Counseling, chapter 8). But you'll feel more comfortable if you know what to expect.

ORTHODOX V. ECLECTIC THERAPY: WHICH BRAND WILL YOUR COUNSELOR REALLY USE?

This book has highlighted three of the most popular brands of attachment-based couples therapy being taught to couples therapists in the United States: Imago, Emotion-Focused Therapy for Couples, and the Gottman Method. I have illustrated how each particular method works by providing condensed scenarios that highlight its common procedures. You may be wondering how—or whether—a textbook-type of guide can be applied to a real-life therapy session, and whether it isn't more likely that a therapist who is free to construct his or her own session will simply select the techniques he likes to use from each treatment and omit others that he finds less effective?

As mentioned in the section above, you should certainly be sure to ask a prospective couples therapist how orthodox he or she is in using the particular brand of therapy you're seeking. Most therapists are eclectic, meaning they use a blend of methods and can't be categorized as any one brand of therapist. Others will happily tell you, "I'm an Imago therapist," or "I'm a Gottman therapist," and will use those methods exclusively.

If a therapist tells you "I am an eclectic therapist," be sure to assess why. I've found that calling oneself "eclectic" can be interpreted as two very different things by prospective clients: 1) "This person must be highly experienced, enough so that he is facile with many techniques and can use them competently when needed," or 2) "This person is inexperienced and is trying to stay in business by not excluding any customers."

To make things even more complicated, some therapists may have trained in an attachment-based couples therapy that was not one of The Big Three brands of couples therapy described earlier in this book. Bear in mind that The Big Three are included in this guide because they are the largest and most organized of the post-graduate training programs available to therapists. Many fine universities and local relationship centers provide top-notch attachment-based couples therapy training using methods not specifically labeled as one of the Big Three, but these are too numerous to name here. However, any competent therapist should be able to describe to you how their approach relates to or differs from The Big Three. This is again why interviewing a prospective therapist is so important: it will either give you confidence in them or not, and it will help you feel more comfortable from the first session if you know what to expect.

HOW TO AVOID INDIVIDUAL THERAPY THAT UNDERMINES YOUR COUPLES THERAPY

There are many reasons you might need both individual and couples counseling at the same time, and many couples therapists will recommend individual therapy at some point during your sessions together. If there are concerns about physical abuse, violence, or untreated addiction, your therapist may even stop conjoint sessions until your individual treatment has begun. But how do you know if your individual therapist might be undermining your couples therapy?

It's a rule of thumb among most couples therapists that the couples therapist you work with should not also be your individual therapist. Some family counselors don't see this as a big concern, however, and may offer for you to start bringing your partner into therapy with you even if you've had a long relationship with that therapist by yourself. But for the most part this is the exception, not the rule. If your situation requires individual therapy as well as couples therapy, you need to make sure your individual therapist understands the complexity of what you are working through in your relationship therapy. This is especially true if you're working with an attachment-based therapist who may use one of the styles of therapy described in this book. Even though attachment-based couples therapy has been around twenty years now, a large number of therapists do not use "relationship-friendly" individual psychology.

Some individual therapists don't have experience with couples or an educational background in couples therapy. When you complain to your individual therapist about something your spouse just did, the therapist probably isn't going to try to help you and help your relationship. Traditional psychotherapy is mostly all about helping and empowering *you*. Little attention will be given to how your own actions may be causing a chain reaction with your partner—which you inevitably must deal with again in the end. Without your partner present during the session, and without close coordination with your couples therapist, an individual therapist can make the common mistake of demonizing your partner because only one side of the story is being presented. The therapist might cite the *Diagnostic and Statistical Manual of Mental Disorders* (the *DSM)* to do it. "Your husband sounds narcissistic," or "your wife may have borderline personality disorder," may be observations from your therapist to explain the problem you're having. It's also not uncommon for traditional individual therapists to remain completely neutral about saving your relationship, which in my opinion isn't a helpful response from a marriage therapist. An attachment-based couples therapist will typically take a firm stand on behalf of repairing your relationship. These therapists will challenge you both, offering tools to help you fix your part of the relationship by working together because relationships are valuable and worth trying to save.

Some individual therapists are highly trained or experienced in relationship psychology and attachment theory. Finding one while you're also in couples therapy could help you get the most out of both types of therapy—individual and couples. Do a little research about any individual therapist you may be considering to avoid hiring two professionals who may pull you in opposite directions simply by virtue of belonging to different schools of therapy. Be sure to mention your concerns about the compatibility of your individual therapy and your couples therapy to both therapists—and ask them to consult with each other regularly about your treatment plan.

TRUST YOUR GUT

It's critical not to rush into choosing a marriage counselor, even if you urgently need help. There's definitely a risk that couples counseling or individual counseling could make things worse for you if you don't work with a therapist you feel like you can trust or who abides by a philosophy that doesn't resonate with you. Some of the most consistent research about therapy outcomes says that the particular model of therapy matters far less than the personal bond you forge with your therapist.

Trust your gut about signals you get from a new therapist. For example, does he or she take time to answer your questions on the phone before you pay for a first session? Does the therapist start your appointments late, but end on time and charge you for the full session? Don't overlook signals like these—they're indicators of how attentive your therapist is to your needs overall.

Above all, don't be shy about expressing any concerns about the therapy itself to your therapist. Those of us who've had in-depth supervision are used to getting feedback—we will welcome and encourage it because it will help us help you. If your therapist regularly gets defensive or flustered about your feedback, it could be a red flag that indicates inexperience or burnout.

LOVE GOOD, BE WELL: JOIN THE CONVERSATION ONLINE

Perhaps the most important lesson I've learned in my firsthand experiences both as the recipient of couples therapy and as the one delivering it is that there are many ways to love good. There's no perfect formula for making a marriage work. There are many options before you and important choices you have to make to truly get the most from the resources available for your relationship. I hope this book has given you many new ideas and caused you to think carefully about how to obtain the highest quality of professional couples therapy. But by no means is my book the final word on this subject. I learn new and exciting things every day about love and relationships, and I love to share this information on my blog and Facebook page. Please tell others who will benefit from this unique clearinghouse for relationship resources and join me in an ongoing conversation. I welcome your questions and want to hear your story about love under repair. You can find me at: www.LoveGoodBeWell.com.

GLOSSARY OF TERMS

-A-

AASECT: American Association of Sexuality Educators, Counselors and Therapists. AASECT provides rigorous certification and ethics standards for sex therapists or sex educators, and maintains a directory of certified professionals: www. aasect.org.

avatar: The identifying information you create when you join an online forum—a website where people discuss topics related to a central theme, such as relationship issues. Avatars are often pseudonyms, which can allow you to share personal information and receive advice and feedback from others without disclosing your actual identity.

-B-

Behavioral Couples Therapy: One of the earliest and most researched forms of couples therapy, introduced during the 1960s. In behavioral couples therapy, partners learn to be nicer to each other, communicate better, and solve problems by negotiating agreements (contracts) for specific changes in behavior. For example, a common method in behavioral couples therapy is to devise a "quid pro quo" (Latin for "something for something") agreement (i.e., you start doing the dishes in exchange for your husband coming home earlier).

Behavioral health provider: The term that insurance companies use to refer to mental health professionals such as psychotherapists and couples therapists.

"Big Three" Brands of Couples Therapy: The three most prominent and widespread methods of couples therapy being taught to post-graduate psychotherapists today. These include: Emotionally Focused Therapy for Couples, Gottman Method Couples Therapy, and Imago Relationship Therapy. While there are many other important and effective styles of couples therapy, the Big Three are distinct in that they each have highly organized training institutes, each conduct or are beginning to conduct substantial research on their effectiveness, and each have worldwide distribution of public workshops and popular books.

-C-

Caring Behaviors Exercise: An exercise used in Imago Relationship Therapy that asks couples to identify the caring behaviors they used to engage in but have stopped doing for each other; couples agree to gradually restart the most readily achievable behaviors again.

counseling: A generic term that means a meeting for the

purposes of receiving advice or information, usually from a professional or person in authority. (See also *psychotherapy*.)

codependent: A term used to label a person's emotional attachment to another as unhealthy as an alcoholic's need for a drink. The idea of codependency was developed to describe the way partners and families of addicts behave in concert, to co-create conditions that support using drugs or alcohol. The codependency movement has been quite helpful to a lot of people and continues to be an important part of treating addiction in families. However, when applied broadly to *all* people, the concepts of codependency can be toxic to efforts to improve relationships. (See also *relational psychology*.)

Conscious Partnership: A term used in Imago Relationship Therapy. In a conscious partnership, partners attempt to end all forms of criticism and avoidance of intimacy and instead make a thoughtful effort to act in ways that build and support each other's emotional needs and dreams.

Cognitive-Behavioral Therapy: Cognitive-Behavioral Therapy (CBT) refers to several specific types of therapy that focus on changing thoughts in order to change feelings or behavior (for example depressed feelings). Brands of CBT include Rational-Emotive Behavior Therapy (REBT), Rational Behavior Therapy (RBT), Rational Living Therapy, Cognitive Therapy, Dialectical Behavior Therapy (DBT), Behavioral Couples Therapy (BCT), and Integrative Behavioral Couples Therapy (IBCT). All cognitive-behavioral therapies traditionally assert that thoughts create feelings and behavior. Interventions focus on using rational capacity to alter thoughts.

CPT Code: *See procedure code.*

-D-

deductible: The dollar amount you must pay out-of-pocket to a health service provider, such as a psychotherapist, during one calendar year before insurance coverage will begin to reimburse you for claims made after the deductible amount is met.

diagnosis code: A five-digit number that corresponds to a mental health diagnosis, according to the *Diagnostic and Statistical Manual of Mental Disorders* (DSM). The latest DSM revision was completed in 2013, and is known as the *DSM-5*. Your therapist may use a DSM diagnosis code for his or her own assessment of your treatment. Many psychotherapists in private practice find these codes increasingly irrelevant to actual treatment of clients and only use them to facilitate coordination of care between providers (especially in inpatient facilities or for substance abuse/mental illness treatment) or for insurance purposes.

discernment counseling: A special type of counseling designed for "mixed-agenda" couples, partners who differ in opinion about the desired outcome of the relationship—to stay together or break up. Created by Dr. William Doherty at the University of Minnesota, discernment counseling has a maximum limit of five sessions. The focus of discernment counseling is not on solving problems in the relationship but on making it clearer for the couple whether or not they want to try to resolve problems or end the relationship.

dyspareunia: Sexual intercourse that is painful. Dyspareunia is more commonly a female condition. It is a condition with many causes, such as a medical condition or physical or emotional trauma. It is treated by specialized sex therapists, gynecologists, and physical therapists.

-E-

eclectic therapist: A psychotherapist that integrates more than one style of therapy in his or her clinical methods.

-F-

Family Systems Therapy: A general term that refers to one of several specific types of psychotherapy that uses principles of systems thinking. Systems thinking evaluates the parts of a system in relation to the whole, and is commonly applied in physics, mathematics, biology, and computing. Systems thinking used in family systems therapy suggests that the behavior of an individual is inseparable from the behavior of the family. If one person in a family changes behavior, it influences the behavior of other members of the family. Specific models of family systems therapy are Structural Family Therapy, Strategic Family Therapy, and Intergenerational Family Therapy. Family systems therapy is often conducted with as many family members involved as possible, but also occurs frequently as a form of individual or couples therapy with a focus on the clients' family of origin.

forum: A website that serves as a gathering place for people interested in sharing experiences about a specific topic. Online forums exist for every imaginable topic, including relationship issues.

fee-for-service practice: A counseling practice that doesn't accept insurance and charges you directly for services. In this kind of practice, the patient is responsible for submitting any claims to an insurance carrier for out-of-network benefits.

Four Horsemen of the Apocalypse: The four behaviors or emotions that, according to Dr. John Gottman, predict "marital doom," or divorce. They are: Criticism, Contempt, Defensiveness, and Stonewalling. Dr. Gottman found that while these are demonstrated by couples that later divorce, seeking professional couples therapy can teach couples to avoid exhibiting each of these four behaviors and save a marriage in distress.

-G-

group couples therapy: A form of couples therapy in which a group of six to ten couples meet with a therapist regularly to focus on the relationship concerns of each couple.

-H- *There are no entries for the letter H.*

-I-

in-network benefit: An insurance benefit that pays for doctors or therapist visits, partially or in full. The service provider submits a claim to an insurance company and the patient/

client pays only a small copay (usually $10–$30) at each visit. All health insurance plans have in-network benefits. A plan that limits participants to in-network providers exclusively is called a Health Maintenance Organization (HMO).

insurance panel: The roster of behavioral health or health providers that members of an insurance company may choose from to receive "in-network" benefits.

Intentional Couple's Dialogue: The primary skill taught to couples in Imago Relationship Therapy. Intentional dialogue asks partners to take turns being a "listener" and a "sender." In Imago therapy, intentional dialogue is used especially to reduce defensive reactions (secondary emotions) and to increase attachment-stimulating primary emotions (feelings that express some vulnerability).

Internal Family Systems (IFS) Therapy: A method of psychotherapy practiced by the author. IFS is a blend of mindfulness, systems thinking, and attachment-based methods, and may be used both with individuals and couples.

-J through L – *There are no entries for letters J–L.*

-M-

marathon couples therapy: A rare, specialized form of couples therapy in which you and your partner meet privately with a therapist for a short but continuous period of time, usually over the course of successive days. Marathon couples therapy is often structured so that you complete an abridged version of a normally 4–8 week course during a period of 12–20 hours over two days.

mental health disciplines: The academic fields of study that, collectively, train people in the field of mental health, which may include practice as a psychotherapist or counselor. An advanced degree (master's level or higher) is required for state licensure from a board of health to practice as a mental health clinician. These academic fields include: counseling (professional counselors), marriage and family therapy (MFT), social work (MSW), psychology, and psychiatry (a medical degree).

mindfulness: A psychological approach often used to reduce stress, depression, and anxiety-based emotions. It's based on nonreligious Buddhist concepts of turning attention inward in a focused and nonjudgmental way. Independent of religious teaching, mindfulness has been popularized in the West by medical-based research and the teachings of Jon Kabat-Zinn, the creator of Mindfulness-Based Stress Reduction (MBSR) and a professor at the University of Massachusetts Medical School.

-N-

neurobiology: The study of the brain and nervous system. A neurobiological approach to psychology incorporates so-called "brain science" with the study of human behavior.

-O-

organic search results: The results from an online search that are based on the online reputation of that website. If a website occupies the first pages of a list of organic search results, it's considered highly relevant to the search term that you entered because of the content of that site and the number of other similar sites that are linked to it. (See also *paid search results*.)

out-of-network benefit: The type of health insurance benefit that pays for doctors or therapist visits, partially or in full, and requires the patient/client to submit an insurance claim and pay the fee-for-service provider upfront. Health insurance plans with out-of-network benefits are either POS (point of service) plans, or PPO (preferred provider organization or participating provider organization).

-P-

paid search results: A paid advertisement that lists a service in online search results. Paid ads usually occupy the first two or three listings at the top of any search results page and those along the right side. (See also *organic search results*.)

premarital counseling: Sometimes called pre-marriage counseling or pre-engagement counseling, premarital counseling is a type of couples therapy for engaged couples or couples considering marriage.

prepare/enrich: A customized couples assessment completed online that identifies a couple's strengths and potential growth areas. It's one of the most widely used materials in premarital counseling and premarital education. Prepare/Enrich is also used for marriage counseling, marriage enrichment, and for dating couples considering engagement. Based on a couple's assessment results, a trained facilitator provides four to eight feedback sessions in which he or she helps the couple discuss and understand their results as they are taught relationship skills.

primary emotions: A term used in Emotionally Focused Therapy (EFT) for couples that describes a person's "soft," vulnerable side. Primary emotions are gut-level feelings not always consciously identified. The most common primary emotions are: hurt, shame, sadness, excitement, joy, and surprise. These emotions have the most potential to stimulate active attachment, or bonding, between you and your partner (see also secondary emotions).

positive psychology: A branch of psychological study that focuses on strengths instead of weakness. In contrast, traditional psychology has historically been the study of mental illness and psychological problems. Positive psychology is known for the study of psychological wellness. The popularity of life coaching and relationship coaching, based largely on positive psychology ideas, has paralleled the rapid growth of interest in positive psychology since the 1990s.

psychoanalytic therapy (psychoanalysis): A form of psychotherapy that places emphasis on the interaction between a person's conscious and subconscious minds. Psychoanalytic therapy, sometimes called psychodynamic therapy, originated with Sigmund Freud in the late 1800s. It has since evolved to encompass at least twenty-two distinct styles. One of the most distinct features of psychoanalytic therapy is the relatively impersonal demeanor of the therapist. This is done intentionally, in an effort to maintain a "blank slate" that compels the patient to form ideas (ostensibly from the subconscious) about the nature of the analyst. In traditional psychoanalysis, the patient sits on a couch, with his or her back facing the therapist.

psychotherapy: Sometimes referred to simply as "therapy," psychotherapy is a type of counseling specifically undertaken for the purpose of creating desired behavioral, emotional, and/ or relationship changes. It's sometimes used interchangeably with *counseling*, a term that's more general and has more broad uses. Psychotherapy implies that the counselor has taken on the specific responsibility of maintaining a close relationship, and tries to foster the emergence of deep emotional disclosure for the purpose of changing behaviors that interfere with stated goals.

procedure code: Known by insurance carriers as the current procedural terminology (CPT code), it's a five-digit number that identifies the type of services that a health or behavioral health provider delivers. The procedure code is found on invoices from a doctor or therapist and is similar to but distinct from ICD-9 codes (used only in inpatient settings), which identify both the type of service delivered and a medical or mental health diagnosis.

-Q- *There are no entries for the letter Q.*

-R-

relational psychology: Also known as "systems thinking" or "systems theory." The idea that our thoughts, feelings, and behavior are strongly influenced by our relationships, and vice versa. In the 1950s, family therapists Murray Bowen, Jay Haley, Virginia Satir and others began to challenge traditional thinking in psychotherapy, which viewed mental health symptoms as only the result of an individual's innate personality or a person's conflicts with a single caregiver, such as a mother.

relationship coaching: An alternative to couples therapy that may be used in conjunction with couples therapy or alone. Unlike psychotherapists, coaches, broadly referred to as "life coaches," are not regulated by state boards of health. Most coaches tend to emphasize positive psychology—an approach that focuses on finding strengths and solutions (rather than identifying problems), and on living to the fullest potential.

-S-

Seattle Love Lab: Nickname of a studio apartment near the University of Washington famous for being the laboratory where Dr. John Gottman and his associates videotaped couples continuously for twenty-four-hour periods to study their emotional states while collecting biometric data.

secondary emotions: A term used in Emotionally Focused Therapy for couples that describes feelings related to a more immediate, gut-level, primary emotion (see *primary emotions*). Secondary emotions are what most people are talking about when they talk about feelings. Secondary emotions evolved to conceal or protect the more vulnerable, primary feelings from being experienced or noticed by others. Typical secondary emotions are frustration, anger, numbness, guilt, and defensiveness.

self-help: The genre of psychologically themed products published online, in print, and in video or audio form that are designed to be used privately to address a specific concern, such as relationship distress.

sensate focusing: A common exercise given to couples during sex therapy that asks them to experiment with pleasurable, nongenital touch in order to eliminate pressure to perform or hurry sexual intimacy.

sex therapy: A specialized psychotherapy (talk therapy) that focuses on improving sexual functioning for a couple or individual. Sex therapists are specifically trained in behavioral modification techniques to help eliminate behaviors that interfere with full sexual functioning and encourage behaviors that promote full sexual functioning. Many sex therapists are also skilled at couples therapy, but this is not universally true. There is no physical contact involved in sex therapy provided by licensed practitioners.

sexologist: A person involved in the scientific study of human sexual interests, behavior, and functioning. A sexologist may also be a sex therapist or personal coach/consultant, though the term refers only to someone who researches or teaches about knowledge pertaining to human sexuality.

Solution-Focused Brief Therapy: Solution-Focused Brief Therapy (SFBT) is an approach used in psychotherapy and life coaching that focuses primarily on goals instead of problems or symptoms. SFBT uses techniques influenced by positive psychology designed to keep the client's attention on the present and future and away from past events. This approach is time-limited and is often clearly defined by the nature of specific and attainable goals.

Sound Relationship House: A Gottman Method concept that describes seven core principles, based on trust and commitment, that couples can use to fend off The Four Horsemen of the Apocalypse and have a successful relationship. (See *Four Horsemen of the Apocalypse.*)

-T-

thread: The term for a series of messages posted by users of an online forum that are related to a single topic.

tracking the cycle: A method used in Emotionally Focused Therapy for couples in which you or your therapist identifies the sequence of defensive and unproductive behaviors in your relationship and replaces them with communication that creates emotional bonds. Tracking the cycle is a way to talk about your reactive feelings (secondary emotions) without being swept up in actually feeling or acting out of those emotions.

troll: The term for a person in an online forum who violates that website's forum rules by posting inappropriate remarks, such as comments intended to demean or personally attack others. Trolls are usually "moderated" on reputable forums, meaning such posts are usually removed by a site administrator, and the person posting is given a warning or banned from the site.

-U-

utilization review: An insurance company's request for your therapy diagnosis and treatment plan for the purposes of justifying or denying continued financial reimbursement for services.

-W-

weekend intensive: Also known as a weekend retreat or weekend workshop. A two- or three-day event for couples seeking to improve their relationship. Weekend intensives are offered by each of the Big Three brands of couples therapy described in this book (as well as many others), and usually consist of educational lectures, video presentations, and private time for reflection and discussion with your partner.

-X through Z- *There are no entries for letters X-Z.*

APPENDIX B:
MENTAL HEALTH PROFESSIONALS: WHO THEY ARE AND HOW TO FIND ONE

Reprinted with permission from National Alliance on Mental Illness (NAMI) www.nami.org

Mental health services are provided by several different professions, each of which has its own training and areas of expertise. Finding the right professional(s) for you or a loved one can be a critical ingredient in the process of diagnosis, treatment and recovery when faced emotional distress or symptoms of serious mental illness.

Types of Professionals Who Provide Mental Health Services:

- **Psychiatrist** – Psychiatrists are physicians with either a doctor of medicine (MD) degree or doctor of osteopathy (DO) degree, who also have at least four additional years of specialized study and training in psychiatry. Psychiatrists are licensed as physicians to practice medicine by individual states. "Board Certified" psychiatrists have passed the national examination administered by the American Board of Psychiatry and Neurology. Psychiatrists provide medical and psychiatric evaluations, treat psychiatric disorders, provide psychotherapy, and prescribe and monitor medications. There are several subspecialty boards in psychiatry including child and adolescent, forensic, and addiction.

- **Psychologist** – Psychologists have a doctoral degree (PhD, PsyD or EdD) in clinical, educational, counseling, or research psychology. Psychologists are also licensed by individual states to practice psychology. They can provide psychological testing, evaluations, treat emotional and behavioral problems and mental disorders, and provide a variety of psychotherapeutic techniques.

- **Psychiatric/Mental Health Nurse Practitioner** – Psychiatric/mental health nurse practitioners (PMHNP) have a four-year college degree in nursing (BSN) and also complete an approved masters of science in nursing (MSN) or doctor of nursing practice (DNP). PMHNPs are licensed by individual states and in some states are required to practice under the supervision of a psychiatrist. PMHNPs provide a wide range of services to adults, children, adolescents, and families including assessment and diagnosis, prescribing medications, and providing therapy for individuals with psychiatric disorders or substance abuse problems.

- **Psychiatric/Mental Health Nurse** – Psychiatric/mental health nurses may have various degrees ranging from associate's (RN) to bachelor's (BSN) to master's (MSN or APRN) to doctoral (DNSc, PhD). Depending on their level of education and licensing, they provide a broad range of psychiatric and medical services, including the assessment and treatment of psychiatric illnesses, case management, and psychotherapy. In certain states, some psychiatric nurses may prescribe and monitor medication.

- **Social Worker** – Social workers have either a bachelor's degree (BA, BS or BSW), a master's degree (MA, MS, MSW or MSSW), or doctoral degree (DSW or PhD). In most states, social workers take an examination to be licensed to practice social work (LCSW or LICSW), and the type of license depends on their level of education and practice experience. Social workers provide a range of services based on their level of training and certification. Typically a bachelor's-level social worker provides case management, inpatient discharge planning services, placement services, and a variety of other daily living needs services for individuals. Master's-level social workers can provide this level of services, but are also able to provide assessment and treatment of psychiatric illnesses, including psychotherapy.

- **Licensed Professional Counselors** – Licensed professional counselors have a master's degree (MA or MS) in psychology, counseling, or other mental health–related fields and typically have two years of supervised post-graduate experience. They may provide services that include assessment and diagnosis of mental health conditions as well as providing individual, family, or group therapy. They are licensed by individual states and may also be certified by the National Board of Certified Counselors.

- **Peer Specialists** – The recognition that peers can offer a unique window into the recovery process is gaining traction across the nation. Learning from someone who "has been there" is often quite helpful. Certification typically occurs on a state-by-state basis, and reimbursement is also locally driven. Contact your local state mental health authority (http://findtreatment.samhsa.gov/MHTreatmentLocator/faces/quickSearch.jspx) to find out where to connect to peer specialists in your state.

- **Certified Alcohol and Drug Counselors** – CADCs are certified individuals who have expertise in working with people who have substance-abuse issues. These providers may have other degrees (e.g., MSW) and have an interest in this area. Substance counseling certifications vary by state.

Resources for Locating a Mental Health Professional

The following sources may help you locate a mental health professional or treatment facility to meet your needs:

- **American Psychiatric Association (APA)** – The APA can give you names of APA members in your area. Find your state branch online at www.psych.org, consult your local phone book, or call (703) 907-7300.

- **American Psychological Association (APA)** – The APA can refer you to local psychologists. Call (800) 374-2721.

- **Insurance Providers** – Contact your insurance company for a list of mental health care providers included in your insurance plan.

- **NAMI State Organizations and NAMI Affiliates** – Speaking with NAMI members (individuals living with mental illness and family members) can be a good way to exchange information about mental health professionals in your local community. You can find your state or local NAMI organization at www.nami.org.

- **National Association of Social Workers (NASW)** – NASW has an online directory of clinical social workers. Visit www.socialworkers.org and click on 'Resources' or call (202) 408-8600.

- **Primary Care Physician (PCP)** – Your primary physician or pediatrician is an excellent resource for making recommendations and referrals to a mental health specialist or therapist in your area.

- **Psychiatry Departments** – Contact local teaching hospitals or medical schools for referrals or information.

- **Substance Abuse and Mental Health Services Administration's (SAMHSA) Center for Mental Health Services** – SAMHSA has an online database of mental health and substance abuse services and facilities in each state. Visit www.samhsa.gov/treatment and click on 'Mental Health Services Locator.'

APPENDIX C:

QUESTIONS TO ASK YOUR INSURANCE COMPANY

Increasingly, many couples therapists consider themselves specialists and are leaving insurance networks to provide "fee-for-service" therapy only. This means you must pay out of pocket for your therapy sessions and submit any insurance claims yourself, if you have an out-of-network benefit. Some fee-for-service practices will submit these claims for you. Either way, it's essential to research your health insurance benefits carefully to determine how much your therapy will cost. The following worksheet is a guide to help you collect the needed information from your insurance company about your medical benefits that may cover psychotherapy, including couples therapy.

1. What is my co-pay? $ _____
   or co-insurance? _____

2. Do I have a deductible for mental health benefits? Yes / No

3. How much of my deductible have I already met this calendar year? _____

4. Are there a maximum number of yearly visits allowed? Yes / No; if yes, how many _____

5. Does your plan have a lifetime maximum mental health benefit? Yes / No Amount _____

6. Does your plan require pre-authorization for mental health benefits? Yes / No

7. Authorization #: _____
   Start Date: _____
   End Date: _____

Authorization details & coverage:

Inquire about whether the following CPT (procedure) codes—that may be used by your therapist—are covered by your plan. The most commonly used CPT code for couples therapy is 90847.

90791 Initial Evaluation   Yes / No

90832 Psychotherapy, 30 minutes with patient and/or family member   Yes / No # of visits allowed: _____

90834 Psychotherapy, 45 minutes with patient and/or family member   Yes / No # of visits allowed: _____

90837 Psychotherapy, 60 minutes with patient and/or family member   Yes / No # of visits allowed: _____

90845 Psychoanalysis   Yes / No # of visits allowed: _____

90846 Family psychotherapy without the patient present

Yes / No # of visits allowed: _____

90847 Family psychotherapy, conjoint psychotherapy with the patient present   Yes / No # of visits allowed: _____

90849 Multiple-family group psychotherapy

Yes / No # of visits allowed: _____

90853 Group psychotherapy (other than of a multiple-family group)   Yes / No # of visits allowed: _____

The following information will help you understand what to expect from your insurance company:

1. It will take approximately 2-3 weeks from the time of your visit for the insurance claim to be received by the insurance company and loaded into their claims system

2. If you wish to call your insurance company and get a claim status, please allow 3 weeks before doing so

3. If your claim has not been loaded into your insurance company's claim system after 3 weeks, resubmit the claim

4. To file a claim yourself, call the number on the back of your insurance card to obtain the necessary information for filing

5. Once your company receives your claim, it may take 30-45 days for a check to be mailed to you

AFTERWORD

AS A STUDENT and teacher of many models of psychotherapy, I found it difficult to stick to my original plan of writing about only the "Big Three" models of couples therapy—Emotionally Focused Therapy for Couples, the Gottman Method Couples Therapy, and Imago Relationship Therapy. For example, although I'm a certified Imago therapist, I've relied on other models of therapy to inform my complex work with couples. Many of my colleagues who are certified practitioners in EFT or the Gottman method have described their journey in how they practice similarly.

My early drafts of *Love Under Repair* included so many references to various methodologies that one of my friends told me it was far too technical to be useful for the average person who simply wanted to understand the general landscape of couples therapy before sitting down on a therapist's couch. In the end my personal experience with wading through couples therapy options convinced me to keep it simple and focus on the Big Three.

Here are a few other methods that are also quite useful, but weren't mentioned in this book:

Internal Family Systems (IFS) Therapy
www.SelfLeadership.org
Schwartz, Richard C. *You Are the One You've Been Waiting For: Bringing Courageous Love to Intimate Relationships*. Oak Park, Ill.: Trailheads, 2008.

Integrative Behavioral Couples Therapy (IBCT)
www.DrAndrewChristensen.com
Christensen, Andrew. *Reconcilable Differences: Rebuild Your Relationship by Rediscovering the Partner You Love—without Losing Yourself.* New York: The Guilford Press, 2014.

Pragmatic/Experiential Therapy for Couples (PET-C)
www.TheCouplesClinic.com
Atkinson, Brent J. *Emotional Intelligence in Couples Therapy: Advances from Neurobiology and the Science of Intimate Relationships.* New York: W.W. Norton, 2005.

Psychobiological Approach to Couples Therapy (PACT)
www.ThePactInstitute.com
Tatkin, Stan. *Wired for Love: How Understanding Your Partner's Brain and Attachment Style Can Help You Defuse Conflict and Build a Secure Relationship.* Oakland, CA: New Harbinger Publications, 2011.

ACKNOWLEDGMENTS

WITHOUT A DOUBT, this book couldn't have been written without my wife. You are truly an anchor for me. Even more amazing is your courageous willingness to trust me to share our story with the world.

I'd like to acknowledge the team of counselors that make up Keith Miller & Associates Counseling. There is enough insight, skill, and compassion within each of these talented individuals to fill the pages of a hundred books.

To Lisa Tenner, for inviting me to the Harvard Medical School Writing and Publishing Workshop and for graciously lending her two cents about all things publishing.

To my editor, Kelly Malone, for coaxing me to climb the steep hills in my manuscript and for being such a strong and steady voice that never let me doubt I could hammer out this whole thing. Your attention to both the nitty-gritty and the big picture was a huge gift—you kept me from going completely off the trail.

Jeremy Bielawski is one of the most talented videographers on the planet. Thank you for jumping into my Kickstarter campaign with enthusiasm and faith. To Joe Petrucci, for brandishing his hidden acting talent and surgical skill. To all 112 backers of my Kickstarter campaign for helping me attempt to reach my goal of crowdfunding the publication of this book—especially my parents, David Sternberg, Anne and David Swisher, Maryrita Wieners, John and Sue Lindsay, Joe Petrucci, and Kathy McMahon. And to my brother, Craig, for helping me keep an entrepreneur's attitude to taking on a big challenge and spending money I didn't have.

To the many friends and colleagues who took the time to carefully read the early drafts and offer encouragement and thoughtful feedback: Joe Bavonese, Tina Payne Bryson, William Doherty, Jay Earley, Dan Erb, Patricia Gibberman, Paul Greenman, Grace Herrle, Brad Hopewell, Deborah Ross, Stacy Notaras Murphy, Jen Kogan, Wade Luquet, Cindy and Daniel Menz-Erb, Jette Simon, Curt Thompson, and Scott Wolfe. Matthew Green deserves special credit for line-editing the manuscript in his sleep while simultaneously grading piles of college essays, writing his own book, and putting his kids to bed.

To Harville and Helen Hendrix, John and Julie Gottman, and Susan Johnson for leading the way in adult attachment long before it was popular. To the creators and teachers of the many other wonderful methods of couples therapy that were beyond the scope of this book. And to my teachers in IFS, Toni Hermine-Blank, Jay Earley, Pamela Krause, and Richard Schwartz—without IFS and your passion for teaching a revolutionary way of doing attachment work with our "inner family" of parts, I don't think I would have been able to separate the forest for the trees and see the need for this book.

274 | LOVE UNDER REPAIR

INDEX

CPSIA information can be obtained at www.ICGtesting.com
Printed in the USA
LVOW01s0246240715

447468LV00026B/383/P